6-3 and 5-4
Betrayal From Within

Barry Robbins

© **2025 Barry Robbins. All rights reserved.**

No portion of this book may be reproduced, in whole or in part, without written permission from the publisher, except for brief excerpts used in reviews.

This book blends factual summaries of U.S. Supreme Court decisions with creative nonfiction techniques, including dramatic voice, metaphor, and personification. These elements are expressive devices, not factual claims about the internal thoughts, motives, or statements of any person, Justice, or institution. The author does not purport to know or represent the subjective beliefs or private intentions of any individual.

This book is intended for informational and educational purposes only, and does not constitute legal advice.

Dedication

This book is dedicated to Pam, my caregiver extraordinaire, without whom this book would not be possible.

Contents

Introduction	1
Prologue — Marbury v. Madison (1803)	5
Individual Rights	9
1. Dobbs v. Jackson Women's Health Organization (2022)	11
2. Salinas v. Texas (2013)	16
3. United States v. Skrmetti (2025)	20
Voting Rights/Elections	25
4. Bush v. Gore (2000)	27
5. Citizens United v. FEC (2010)	32
6. Arizona Free Enterprise Club v. Bennett (2011)	37
7. Shelby County v. Holder (2013)	43
8. Rucho v. Common Cause (2019)	48
9. Brnovich v. Democratic National Committee (2021)	54
Regulatory/Administrative	59

10. West Virginia v. EPA (2022)	61
11. Loper Bright Enterprises v. Raimondo (2024)	66
Religion	**71**
12. Burwell v. Hobby Lobby Stores (2014)	73
13. 303 Creative LLC v. Elenis (2023)	78
14. Kennedy v. Bremerton School District (2022)	84
15. Carson v. Makin (2022)	88
16. Mahmoud v. Taylor (2025)	93
Second Amendment	**99**
17. District of Columbia v. Heller (2008)	101
18. New York State Rifle & Pistol Association v. Bruen (2022)	111
Civil Rights	**117**
19. Parents Involved in Community Schools v. Seattle School District No. 1 (2007)	119
20. Students for Fair Admissions v. President and Fellows of Harvard College (2023)	124
Labor Rights	**129**
21. Janus v. American Federation of State, County, and Municipal Employees (2018)	131
22. Cedar Point Nursery v. Hassid (2021)	136
Executive Power	**141**

23.	Trump v. Hawaii (2018)	143
24.	Trump v. CASA, Inc. (2025)	148
25.	Trump v. United States (2024)	153
Also by Barry Robbins		159
About the author		161

Introduction

The Supreme Court is supposed to be the conscience of the nation — the one place where principle survives politics, where rights outlast elections. Or so we tell ourselves.

For most of my life, I believed that story. The marble columns, the robes, the solemn language — all of it suggested something higher, something apart from the raw power of ordinary politics. But over the past twenty-five years, that illusion has shattered. Case by case, decision by decision, the Court has rewritten the meaning of freedom, equality, and government itself.

What was once a shield for the vulnerable has become a weapon for the powerful.

Every case in this book begins with people — a woman, a worker, a voter, a teacher. Then the Court speaks, and the people disappear into doctrine. The opinions grow longer, the footnotes more intricate, the reasoning more detached. The law becomes a language only lawyers understand, and justice retreats into abstraction.

This book tries to bring the people back.

Each chapter gives voice to a case — not the judges, not the lawyers, but the thing itself. A ballot that never got counted. A taxpayer dollar forced to fund a sermon. A union fee that can no longer be collected. The Constitution itself, bewildered at what's been done in its name. These are the voices of the decisions that reshaped modern America — not as legal arguments, but as lived consequences.

The cases that follow share a pattern. They were all decided in the twenty-first century. They were all close — five-to-four, then six-to-three as the Court shifted. And together they trace the arc of something that once seemed impossible: the internal undoing of American constitutional progress.

Marbury v. Madison gave the Court its power. *Dobbs v. Jackson Women's Health Organization* showed what that power could destroy. Between them lies more than two centuries of faith that law could protect the powerless from politics. That faith is what this book mourns.

I'm not a constitutional scholar. This isn't a textbook or a legal commentary. It's a reckoning — a record of how the Court's majority has turned words like "liberty," "equal protection," and "religious freedom" into instruments of exclusion. The tone is unapologetically biased, because neutrality in the face of injustice isn't virtue; it's surrender.

Each voice in these pages asks you to feel what the Court refused to see. The hollow sound of rights being narrowed. The quiet violence of reasoning that closes doors instead of opening them. The human cost behind each citation and clause.

The Supreme Court doesn't act in sudden revolutions. It erodes. It chips away. One precedent at a time, one quiet footnote at a time, until what once was solid becomes air.

This book begins where that erosion shows most clearly — in *Dobbs*, where fifty years of reproductive freedom vanished overnight. From there, the stories unfold across voting rights, free speech, religion, guns, labor, and power itself. The pattern is unmistakable: decisions that claim to defend freedom by restricting it, that praise equality while dismantling it, that quote *Brown v. Board* to justify segregation's return.

The Court's majority tells us that the Constitution means what it says. Maybe so. But it's worth asking who gets to say what it means — and who pays the price when they do.

Here are twenty-five answers.

Prologue — Marbury v. Madison (1803)

I am Judicial Review, and I was born in 1803 in a case that wasn't supposed to change the world.

On the surface, *Marbury v. Madison* was about one man — William Marbury — and a commission that never reached him. President John Adams, in his final hours in office, had appointed Marbury as a justice of the peace. The paperwork was signed, sealed, but undelivered when Thomas Jefferson took over. Jefferson told his Secretary of State, James Madison, not to deliver it. Marbury sued, demanding the Supreme Court make Madison hand it over.

That was the immediate drama. But in the background, Chief Justice John Marshall was quietly sketching out something much larger than one commission.

Marshall's opinion said two things:
  1. Yes, Marbury was entitled to his commission.

  2. No, the Court couldn't give it to him—because the law that would have allowed the Court to do so was itself unconstitutional.

And here's where I was born. For the first time, the Supreme Court declared that it had the power to strike down a law passed by Congress if that law violated the Constitution. Marshall wrote it plainly: *It is emphatically the province and duty of the judicial department to say what the law is.*

That single sentence was my first breath.

Before me, the Court was respected but not supreme. Congress made laws, the President enforced them, and the Court was a quieter partner in the system. After me, I had the power to decide which laws lived and which died.

I was elegant. I was logical. I was, at first, a humble servant—a safeguard to ensure that the Constitution meant something real. And for much of my youth, I served well. I protected rights. I kept the other branches in check. I was the quiet conscience of American law.

But power ages differently than people. It grows heavier over time, more sure of itself. I began to notice how intoxicating my own authority was—how a handful of justices, robed and unelected, could tilt the entire country with a single opinion.

Many years passed, and I watched my wielders change. Some used me to expand freedom—ending segregation, protecting speech, striking down bans on interracial marriage. Others used me to uphold injustice—*Plessy v. Ferguson, Korematsu v. United States*. Each time, my power was the same. Only the hands that held me changed.

By the dawn of the 21st century, I was no longer young, no longer humble. The Court had learned to use me with precision—sometimes for noble ends, sometimes to erase decades of progress. And I could feel a shift: the justices were less bound by restraint, more willing to remake society in their image.

In 1803, I was the careful tool John Marshall crafted to keep the Constitution alive. In 2025, I am the sharpened blade the Court uses to cut away rights that generations had fought to secure.

I think often about that day in the early 19th century. About the candlelight flickering in Marshall's chambers, the scratch of his quill as he drafted the opinion. I wonder if he knew that his words would echo not just through his lifetime, but into centuries he could never imagine—centuries where the country would grow, fracture, and fight over what freedom means.

I wonder if he could see the future, if he would have hesitated. Or if he would have written the same words, trusting that those who came after him would wield me with wisdom.

Sometimes, I wish I could go back to being the quiet safeguard I was meant to be—stepping in only when the law and the Constitution were in true conflict. But I can't unmake myself. I am here, in every term of the Court, in every major decision.

I am Judicial Review. I was born as a principle of balance. I have become the instrument of both liberation and oppression. And in the chapters ahead, you will see what happens when the balance tilts, when my power falls into hands that value ideology over humanity.

The cases that follow are my children, too—the product of the power John Marshall gave me more than two centuries ago.

Some will break your heart. Some will make you furious. All will remind you of one thing: I am still here, and I am still deciding what the law is.

INDIVIDUAL RIGHTS

Chapter 1
Dobbs v. Jackson Women's Health Organization (2022)

Mississippi passed a law banning most abortions after 15 weeks of pregnancy, directly challenging Roe v. Wade's framework that protected abortion rights until fetal viability (around 24 weeks). The state explicitly asked the Supreme Court to overturn Roe, arguing that the Constitution contains no right to abortion and that states should be free to regulate or ban the procedure as they see fit.

The Supreme Court ruled 6-3 to uphold Mississippi's law and 5-4 to overturn Roe v. Wade entirely. Justice Alito's majority opinion declared that the Constitution contains no right to abortion, that Roe was "egregiously wrong from the start," and that the issue should be left to elected legislators in each state. The majority argued that Roe lacked historical foundation and that abortion rights weren't "deeply rooted" in American legal tradition. The decision eliminated federal constitutional protection for abortion access, allowing states to ban the procedure entirely. The dissenters warned that the majority was abandoning decades of precedent and that no constitutional right was safe if the Court could simply declare past decisions wrong based on the personal views of current justices.

Majority: Thomas, Alito, Gorsuch, Kavanaugh, Barrett, Roberts
Dissent: Breyer, Sotomayor, Kagan

****

I am a uterus, and they just made me property of the state.

For forty-nine years, I belonged to the woman who carried me. Her choices about what happened inside my walls were hers to make. Her decisions about pregnancy, about timing, about her body's future—those were private matters between her and her conscience, her and her doctor, her and her God if she chose.

I was her sanctuary. Her domain. Her body.

Now I belong to politicians.

I feel the shift in my very tissue, in the blood that flows through my arteries, in the hormones that pulse through my chambers. Something fundamental has changed. The autonomy I once knew—the sovereignty I took for granted—has been stripped away with the stroke of judicial pens.

Six justices looked at me and decided I was not my owner's to control. That my function, my purpose, my monthly rhythms should be subject to legislative oversight. That what grows within my walls belongs more to the state than to the woman who houses me.

I am ancient. I have existed in countless forms across countless women for thousands of years. I have carried wanted pregnancies to term with joy. I have expelled unwanted pregnancies with relief.

I have mourned miscarriages with grief. I have celebrated births with triumph. Always, always, these experiences belonged to the women who carried me.

Until now.

Justice Alito held the scalpel that severed my connection to my owner's sovereignty. He declared that I had never truly belonged to her at all—that the Constitution contained no protection for her control over my function. That forty-nine years of precedent recognizing her dominion over my chambers was "egregiously wrong from the start."

I felt myself being dissected by his words, examined like a specimen in a laboratory rather than a living part of a living woman. He studied my history, my legal standing, my constitutional protection—and found me wanting. Not deeply rooted enough in American tradition. Not explicitly mentioned in eighteenth-century documents. Not worthy of continued autonomy.

The cruelest cut was his claim that returning control over me to legislators was somehow democratic. As if my owner's most intimate decisions about her body should be subject to majority vote. As if reproductive choices should be decided in state capitals by people who will never carry pregnancies, never face the physical and emotional weight of what happens inside my walls.

I know what's coming. I feel it in the tremors that run through my tissue, in the fear that constricts my blood vessels. Across the country, my sisters are already experiencing the new reality. In Texas, we're monitored for signs of pregnancy like surveillance equipment. In Missouri, we're forbidden from ending pregnancies even when they threaten our owner's life. In Louisiana, we're forced to carry pregnancies to term regardless of fetal viability.

We've become crime scenes. Evidence in potential prosecutions. Weapons turned against the women who house us.

I remember the time before Roe, when women whispered about coat hangers and kitchen tables, about dangerous procedures in unsafe places. When desperate women risked death rather than carry unwanted pregnancies. When I became a battlefield where women fought for control of their own bodies, often losing their lives in the process.

The majority pretended that returning to those days was somehow progress. That stripping away constitutional protection was a victory for democracy. That forcing women to seek abortions in other states—or risk illegal procedures—was a reasonable compromise.

But I know better. I've felt the panic that floods my owner's bloodstream when she misses a period and can't afford another child. I've experienced the relief when she had options, when she could make decisions about her future without facing criminal prosecution. I've lived through the terror of unwanted pregnancy in a world where pregnancy equals legal captivity.

The dissenters understood. Justices Breyer, Sotomayor, and Kagan saw what the majority refused to acknowledge—that this wasn't just about abortion rights, but about whether women would remain full citizens or become vessels for state reproductive policy. They warned that if constitutional rights could be eliminated simply because current justices disagreed with past decisions, no right was safe.

They were right. If my autonomy could be revoked because Justice Alito found it insufficiently rooted in history, what protection did any privacy right have? What stopped future Courts from declaring that contraception rights, marriage rights, intimate relationship rights were also "egregiously wrong"?

I feel myself becoming a contested territory. Politicians campaign on controlling me. Legislators debate my function as if they understand my complexity. Prosecutors prepare to criminalize my owner's choices as if reproductive decisions were matters of criminal law rather than medical care.

The woman who carries me tries to comfort me, to tell me that nothing has changed, that I'm still hers. But we both know that's not true anymore. Every month when her cycle begins, we both wonder if this will be the month that brings an unwanted pregnancy she can't legally end. Every intimate moment carries new weight, new fear, new calculations about consequences she can no longer control.

I am a uterus, and I used to belong to my owner.
Now I belong to whatever politicians happen to control the legislature in whatever state my owner lives in.
I am no longer part of her body.
I am an instrument of state policy.

And the Supreme Court calls this freedom.

Chapter 2
Salinas v. Texas (2013)

Genovevo Salinas voluntarily answered police questions during a non-custodial interview about a double murder. But when officers asked if shotgun shells found at the crime scene would match his gun, he stopped. For three seconds, he looked down, shifted in his chair, and said nothing.

At trial, prosecutors told the jury that silence was as good as a confession: an innocent man would have denied it immediately. Salinas argued that using his silence against him violated his Fifth Amendment right against self-incrimination.

In a 5–4 decision, the Supreme Court ruled that because Salinas had not been arrested and had not explicitly invoked his Fifth Amendment rights, his silence could be used as evidence of guilt. Justice Alito wrote that in non-custodial situations, the Fifth Amendment must be claimed out loud—simply remaining silent is not enough. The dissent called it a constitutional trap: invoking the Fifth looks suspicious, but failing to invoke it makes your silence fair game for the prosecution.

Majority: Roberts, Scalia, Kennedy, Thomas, Alito
Dissent: Ginsburg, Breyer, Sotomayor, Kagan

****

I am Genovevo's silence, and they turned me into a confession.

For three seconds I hung in that interview room like a bead of sweat on the edge of falling. The air smelled faintly of coffee gone cold. Fluorescent light hummed overhead. Somewhere behind the mirrored wall, a clock ticked, each click of the second hand landing in my bones. Three seconds is nothing in the outside world—long enough to blink twice, to brush a crumb from your shirt. But inside that small, echoing room, three seconds was an eternity.

I wasn't defiance. I wasn't guilt. I was a pause—the most human of responses when a question hits like a blunt instrument: *Would the shotgun shells found at the scene match your gun?*

Genovevo's eyes dropped to the tabletop. His fingers twitched once, then stilled. His foot made a soft scuff on the linoleum. He let me hold the space between question and answer because words, once released, can't be taken back. I was there to give him a heartbeat's safety—a moment to think, to remember, to weigh.

For more than two centuries, that's been my role. I am the Fifth Amendment's living breath: "No person shall be compelled in any criminal case to be a witness against himself." I am the space where compulsion stops and choice begins.

But in that courtroom months later, I stood accused. The prosecutor paced before the jury, his shoes whispering over the carpet. "An innocent man," he said, "would have denied it immediately." Then he stopped—stopped speaking, stopped moving—and let his own silence mimic mine, a performance aimed at twelve strangers in a jury box. "But the defendant said nothing. And that silence speaks volumes."

I wanted to shout. I was not guilt. I was thought. But no one in that room could hear me. The prosecutor painted me as a stain that couldn't be scrubbed away, and the jury leaned forward to see it.

Justice Alito's opinion sealed my fate. He said that because Genovevo had not spoken the magic words—*I invoke my Fifth Amendment right to remain silent*—I could be used against him. A cruel trick: to keep me, you must speak me aloud, but speaking me aloud will look like guilt to the very people judging you.

It was an impossible geometry. Speak and look guilty. Stay quiet and become evidence.

The jurors didn't see hesitation as caution, or fear, or the shock of being accused. They saw what the prosecutor told them to see: guilt. And I watched Genovevo's face when he realized that I, the silence he trusted, had been turned against him. His expression didn't change much—just a small tightening around the mouth—but inside, I felt the collapse.

The dissenters tried to save me. Justice Breyer warned of the trap this created for anyone questioned by police. But dissent is powerless in the moment; it's a candle in a room where the switch has already been flipped to dark.

Now I linger in every police interview room like a shadow with teeth. There is a teenager in Ohio who pauses when an officer asks if the backpack is his. A woman in Florida who freezes when detectives ask about a neighbor's disappearance. A man in Arizona who glances at the floor before answering whether he's been in the alley behind the store. None is under arrest. None has a lawyer beside them. None knows that if they let me carry their hesitation, I might later testify against them.

I remember when I was golden. In the Miranda era, I was untouchable: "You have the right to remain silent." It was recited like a blessing over anyone in handcuffs. I was a line no one could cross.

But *Salinas* dragged me out of that safehouse. Now I am unshielded in the open air, where anyone can twist me into something I am not.

The police know it. The prosecutors know it. And now, anyone who has heard about *Salinas v. Texas* knows it: I am no longer pure protection. I am a gamble.

Picture the interview room again. Genovevo shifts in his chair. The officer waits, pen hovering. The mirror reflects us both, but on the other side, unseen eyes are already thinking about what three seconds of quiet might look like to a jury. In those three seconds, futures pivot. Jobs are lost. Freedom evaporates.

I am not supposed to be a razor blade hidden in the pocket of the Constitution. But that's what the Court made me.

I am Genovevo's silence, and I am no longer your shield.

I am the pause they can prosecute.
The gap they can fill with their own story.

And the Court says that's constitutional law.

And so I live on in the space between question and answer,
Heavier than I used to be,
Sharp-edged where I was once smooth.

I wait, holding my breath for the next person who trusts me—
And I pray they know the risk.

Because now, in America,
Silence is no longer golden.

It's evidence.

Chapter 3
United States v. Skrmetti (2025)

Tennessee passed a law banning gender-affirming medical care for transgender minors, including puberty blockers, hormone therapy, and gender transition surgeries. The law prohibited doctors from providing these treatments to patients under 18, even when recommended by medical professionals and desired by families. The Biden administration and affected families challenged the law as a violation of the Equal Protection Clause and the Due Process Clause, arguing it discriminated based on transgender status and interfered with parental rights and medical decision-making.

The Supreme Court ruled 6–3 to uphold Tennessee's ban, finding that states have broad authority to regulate medical treatments for minors and that the law did not constitute impermissible discrimination. The majority argued that the ban applied equally to all minors regardless of their gender identity, and that states could reasonably conclude that gender-affirming care for children was experimental or potentially harmful. They rejected claims that the law discriminated based on sex or transgender status, characterizing it instead as a neutral regulation of medical procedures. The dissenters argued that the law clearly targeted transgender youth for discriminatory treatment and violated both equal protection principles and fundamental parental rights to make medical decisions for their children.

Majority: Roberts, Thomas, Alito, Gorsuch, Kavanaugh, Barrett
Dissent: Sotomayor, Kagan, Jackson

****

I am a prescription for puberty blockers, and they just made me contraband.

Yesterday, I was medicine. Today, I am evidence of a crime.

Dr. Martinez wrote me carefully, her pen moving across my surface with the practiced precision of someone who had done this a hundred times. The black ink curled and looped in her neat hand, every letter deliberate. She paused twice to check the spelling of my patient's name, and once more to confirm the dosage. My patient was thirteen, pale with anxiety, their leg bouncing under the chair as they spoke in a voice that didn't feel like theirs anymore.

I was hope in pharmaceutical form. A pause button on puberty's machinery. A gift of breathing space—a reprieve from the daily humiliation of watching a stranger's reflection take over the mirror. I wasn't permanent. I wasn't irreversible. I was time—the most precious medicine of all.

But overnight, I became illegal.

The Tennessee legislature decided my molecules were too dangerous for transgender youth—though not, curiously, for any other child. I can still slow puberty for a kid with precocious development. I can still help those whose bodies race ahead too early. But if the same drug, at the same dose, is meant to keep a transgender teen from developing features that cause them distress, I am suddenly forbidden.

The same prescription. The same compound. The same child. Different law.

Six justices of the Supreme Court looked at that difference and declared it "neutral regulation." They said this wasn't discrimination—it was protecting children. Children like mine, apparently, need protection not from their suffering, but from the relief I could bring.

I remember the appointment where Dr. Martinez had to tell my patient's family. The clinic smelled faintly of antiseptic and coffee. The mother's shoulders slumped as if someone had hung weights on them. The father's knuckles went pale against the arm of the chair. The child just stared at the prescription pad, as if I had personally chosen to betray them.

"What happens now?" the mother asked, her voice thin as paper.

Dr. Martinez sighed. "You wait... or you travel... or—" She stopped. The unspoken "or" filled the room like smoke: back channels, risky substitutes, desperate measures.

I was folded into a wallet like a smuggled photograph. At home, they laid me on the kitchen counter under a stack of insurance papers. They debated Illinois versus New Mexico, compared gas prices and airfare. They whispered about cost, about quitting jobs, about leaving grandparents behind. In the next room, my patient sat in silence, feeling their body shift one irreversible notch at a time.

I am not alone in this exile.

In Memphis, another prescription like me lies hidden in a shoebox, written for a boy who can't bear the deepening of his voice. In Knoxville, one gathers dust in a locked desk drawer while a girl counts the weeks until breast growth begins. In rural counties, families without the means to travel watch their children change in ways they begged to stop, while I and my twins sit useless in pockets, drawers, glove compartments.

Dr. Martinez keeps a drawer full of us, all written in good faith, all useless. Pieces of paper that could stop a spiral toward depression, self-harm, or worse—trapped by a law penned by people who have never once held the hand of a crying teenager who just wants their body to make sense.

The Court's majority spoke of "state authority" and "reasonable conclusions" about harm. But they never mentioned the harm of a morning when you wake and your reflection has changed in a way you begged it not to. They didn't speak of the harm of watching your child shrink from family photos, or of marking the calendar not for birthdays but for milestones of unwanted change.

My patient's family checks the mailbox each day for news—legal challenges, injunctions, anything that might free me to do my job. In the meantime, they measure the child's height against the kitchen doorway and pretend not to notice the changes they can't stop.

I am still what I was when I left Dr. Martinez's pen: safe, effective, backed by decades of medical research. The law did not make me dangerous. It simply declared me forbidden for the children who need me most.

I am a prescription for puberty blockers, written with care, requested with love, needed with urgency. And I am contraband.

Not because of science. Not because of safety. But because six justices decided that some children's pain is politically acceptable.

I wait in this wallet, day after day, while the body I was meant to protect is altered beyond recall. I can feel the air around me growing heavier, as if the ink itself knows it is powerless.

Some nights, I imagine a different world—one where I am handed over the pharmacy counter with a smile, where the pharmacist congratulates the family on taking care of their child. Where my patient walks out into the Tennessee sun feeling like the future is theirs again. But morning comes, and I am still here, folded and waiting, while that future slips away.

Medicine turned into contraband.

Hope turned into evidence.

And the Supreme Court calls this protecting children.

VOTING RIGHTS/ ELECTIONS

Chapter 4
Bush v. Gore (2000)

The 2000 presidential election came down to Florida, where George W. Bush led Al Gore by only a few hundred votes out of nearly six million cast. The razor-thin margin triggered an automatic recount. But irregularities abounded: "hanging chads" on punch-card ballots that weren't fully perforated, "butterfly ballots" that confused voters, and inconsistent recount standards from county to county. The Florida Supreme Court ordered a statewide manual recount to resolve the disputes.

Before the process could be completed, the U.S. Supreme Court intervened. In a 5–4 decision, the Court halted the recount, citing the Equal Protection Clause of the Fourteenth Amendment: varying standards across counties meant voters weren't being treated equally. But instead of ordering a fair remedy, the Court stopped the recount altogether—effectively handing the presidency to George W. Bush. In an extraordinary move, the majority declared that their reasoning applied only to this case and set no precedent.

The dissenting justices condemned the majority for abandoning judicial restraint and undermining faith in democracy. They argued the Court should never have intruded into a state electoral process and that by halting the count, the Court itself had chosen the next president.

Majority: Rehnquist, O'Connor, Scalia, Kennedy, Thomas
Dissent: Stevens, Souter, Ginsburg, Breyer

****

I am a Florida ballot, and I never got to speak.

I lived for thirty-six days in a gray metal box, stacked with others like me—thousands of us, each holding the breath of democracy, each waiting to be heard.

I remember election day. Mrs. Rodriguez held me with trembling hands in a West Palm Beach polling station. The air smelled of floor polish and nervous sweat. She squinted at my butterfly design, puzzled by the misaligned columns and tiny circles that seemed meant to trick the eye. Her arthritis made her grip shaky, but she pressed the stylus with all the force she could. The hole didn't quite break free. A hanging chad clung stubbornly, a tiny square of cardboard dangling from my surface.

That hanging chad was my voice. It whispered "Gore" to anyone who cared to look closely. A whisper clear enough for those with patience, magnifying glasses, and honesty. But the louder voices outside the box didn't want to hear whispers. They wanted silence.

For thirty-six days, I felt the country's weight pressing down on my cardboard skin. Crowds chanted in the streets. Lawyers filed motions by the hour. News anchors leaned over maps of Florida, their voices tight with suspense. Inside my box, it was muffled and airless, but we ballots knew what was happening. Some wanted us counted, one by one, under bright lights, so that our meaning could be honored. Others wanted the box sealed forever, our voices stifled.

The Florida Supreme Court ordered that we be examined. For a moment, hope fluttered in my dangling chad. Maybe someone would finally see Mrs. Rodriguez's intent, shaky but clear. Maybe democracy would mean what she thought it meant: that every vote counts, even messy ones.

But hope is fragile.

Far away, nine justices picked up our fate like a toy. Five of them decided that equality demanded silence. They spoke of the Equal Protection Clause, of uniform standards, of fairness. But fairness, it turned out, meant stopping the count altogether. Equality, it turned out, meant treating all of us ballots the same—equally uncounted.

Their words slammed shut the box. "No more counting." With that, my hanging chad fluttered once, then went still. My whisper was drowned out by the gavel.

The cruelty was not in being misread. It was in being deliberately silenced. Not because democracy had broken down, but because democracy was inconvenient. Not because counting was impossible, but because counting was dangerous—it might have changed the outcome.

I was still here, heavy with unspent meaning, when networks declared Bush the winner. I heard fireworks in the night sky, muffled cheers spilling through the streets. I remained unpunched, unresolved, a fragment of Mrs. Rodriguez's faith in the system. That faith now dangled by a thread, just like me.

Years later, journalists and academics counted us properly. They held us up to the light, tilted us this way and that, and finally recognized what we had always said: Gore had more of us than Bush. But by then it was a historical footnote. By then, the presidency had been decided not by ballots but by judges. By then, I was no longer a vote—I was evidence.

Evidence that when democracy becomes too messy, too unpredictable, too threatening to the powerful, it can be stopped by decree. Evidence that the highest court in the land could claim to honor equality while silencing millions. Evidence that votes are fragile things, their power contingent not on ink and cardboard, but on the willingness of those in power to let them matter.

I think about Mrs. Rodriguez sometimes. Did she tell her friends she voted? Did she sit in her kitchen watching the news, waiting for her choice to be honored, unaware that I lay in a box, unheard? Did she know that her ballot, her voice, her belief in democracy had been set aside by five people she would never meet?

I wanted to speak for her. I wanted to shout her choice into the record of history. Instead, I was silenced, my potential stolen, my meaning locked away.

And I know I am not alone. I hear the echoes of future elections, of other voters whose voices falter in the machinery of power. Voter ID laws, gerrymandered districts, purged rolls—different tools, same silencing. Bush v. Gore was only the beginning, the first crack in the foundation. Once the Court showed it could stop votes from being counted, the faith that every voice matters began to wither.

I am a Florida ballot
and I never got to speak.

I am democracy interrupted
suffocated in a metal box while the nation watched.

My hanging chad is still there if you look closely.
It trembles with the weight of what was lost.

And it whispers still: count me. Count me. Count me.

Chapter 5
Citizens United v. FEC (2010)

Citizens United, a conservative nonprofit, wanted to air a film attacking Hillary Clinton in the run-up to the 2008 primaries, but federal law barred corporations from spending money on "electioneering communications" within 30 days of a primary. They sued, claiming the ban violated free speech.

In a 5–4 decision, the Court ruled that corporations have the same First Amendment rights as individuals, striking down limits on independent corporate political spending. Direct contributions to candidates remain capped, but "independent" spending—ads, films, smear campaigns—became limitless. The decision overturned decades of precedent, dismissing the idea that the "appearance of corruption" justified restrictions. Critics warned it opened the floodgates for corporate domination of elections.

Majority: Roberts, Scalia, Kennedy, Thomas, Alito
Dissent: Stevens, Ginsburg, Breyer, Sotomayor

****

6-3 AND 5-4

I am twenty-five dollars, and I just became invisible.

Not in Maria's hands—I'm still green and crisp, still buy groceries or bus fare—but in the democracy where I once mattered, I no longer exist. I am a whisper smothered by a hurricane of corporate shouting.

Maria carried me in her wallet for three weeks like a small treasure. She skipped her morning coffee, packed lunches in Tupperware, walked to work instead of taking the bus. On some days, she'd take me out just to look at me, reminding herself of the purpose I was destined for. She kept me pressed between two old receipts—one from the grocery store, one from the pharmacy—as if I were part of the household budget.

On a rainy Friday night, she sat at the kitchen table with her laptop open, the lamp casting a circle of warm light on the Formica. Her daughter colored in the next room. Maria typed her debit card number into the campaign website, clicked "Donate," and exhaled like she'd just signed a peace treaty.

To most people, I'd be pocket change. To Maria, I was a trade: comfort for conviction.

When I left her account, I wasn't just money. I was her belief that democracy could still be powered by people. I arrived at campaign headquarters alongside a ragtag army—five-dollar bills from ramen-eating students, fifty from retired teachers, a hundred from single mothers who had been setting aside singles in a jar for half a year. Together, we were proof that democracy could be built from the ground up.

Then five justices rewrote the rules.

They decided corporations are people—that ExxonMobil's "voice" deserves the same protection as Maria's. That Walmart's megaphone is just another citizen speaking freely. They called it free speech, as if drowning out human voices wasn't censorship at all.

The day the decision came down, I shrank. Not in size, but in meaning. While Maria counts pennies, corporations can spend millions without blinking. What takes her three weeks of sacrifice, they can drop like loose change under a boardroom table.

The first wave came fast. Television screens lit up with attack ads—slick, relentless, impossible to avoid. They were bankrolled by "Americans for Prosperity" and other shadowy fronts with names designed to sound like your friendly neighbor. The lies were easy to spot if you knew the truth, but they were repeated at a volume that made them sound inevitable.

At the campaign office, volunteers stopped smiling as the ad buys grew heavier. Sam, a college kid with a mop of hair in his eyes, brought in a crumpled envelope from his grandmother's Social Security check. "She wants to help," he said. I sat in Maria's purse next to his donation. Neither of us would matter.

On election night, Maria's living room was quiet. Her daughter fell asleep on the couch with the TV's blue light flickering over her face. Maria sat still, hands clasped so tightly her knuckles whitened, as the results rolled in. Her candidate lost in a landslide. The victor promised tax cuts for corporations and smiled for cameras flanked by factory owners.

"My vote didn't matter," Maria whispered to her daughter, though the girl was still asleep. "None of it mattered."

That's when I understood: the Court hadn't expanded speech. It had sold it. They'd turned democracy into an auction where billionaires are the only bidders. Maria's twenty-five dollars—her lunch breaks, her bus fare, her skipped coffees—was now a quaint relic of an earlier time, like a love letter dropped into a roaring jet engine.

And I wasn't alone.

I thought of Carlos's ten dollars from overtime shifts at the warehouse, meant to support a candidate who promised safer working conditions. I thought of Linda's fifty, scraped together from babysitting gigs, sent to fight for climate action. I thought of Devon's twenty, from his job stocking grocery shelves, intended to protect his union. We were all stripped of our value in the same instant.

Before Citizens United, we had a fighting chance. Candidates could still win on shoe-leather campaigns and grassroots organizing. Ads were expensive, yes, but they had limits. You could knock on enough doors to make up for what you lacked in cash.

After Citizens United, the ground shifted. The doors stayed the same, but the air above them was filled with attack ads, robocalls, and targeted Facebook videos, all crafted by professionals and pumped full of millions in corporate cash. It was no longer a contest of ideas—it was an arms race of wallets.

Maria still sends me out every election cycle. She still believes I might be a seed that grows into change. But the soil is poisoned now. My voice doesn't echo in the town square; it's drowned out by the thunder of corporate jets delivering six-figure checks to private fundraisers.

Sometimes I imagine what it would feel like to be one of those corporate dollars. To glide effortlessly into a Super PAC's war chest. To be multiplied by the millions, unleashed in a flood of attack ads and lobbyist lunches. But then I remember: those dollars have no loyalty, no heartbeat, no Maria behind them. They don't skip coffee for democracy. They skip taxes for profit.

In this new world, Maria's voice—and mine—are still technically "free." But we are free the way a whisper is free in a stadium full of air horns.

Five justices killed her voice.

And called it freedom.

Chapter 6
Arizona Free Enterprise Club v. Bennett (2011)

Arizona created a public campaign financing system where candidates could choose to receive taxpayer funding for their campaigns. To level the playing field, the law provided that when privately-funded opponents (or independent groups supporting them) spent above certain thresholds, publicly-funded candidates would receive additional matching funds. This was designed to prevent wealthy interests from drowning out candidates who relied on public financing.

The Supreme Court ruled 5-4 that the matching funds provision violated the First Amendment rights of privately-funded candidates and independent spenders. The majority argued that the prospect of triggering additional funding for opponents would "chill" the speech of those spending private money, as they would have to consider that their spending might generate matching funds for their political rivals. Chief Justice Roberts wrote that the law created a "substantial burden" on free speech by forcing speakers to internalize the costs of their political expression. The dissenters argued that the law actually enhanced speech by enabling more candidates to participate in political discourse and that wealthy speakers' rights weren't violated simply because their opponents received resources to respond.

Majority: Roberts, Scalia, Kennedy, Thomas, Alito
Dissent: Kagan, Ginsburg, Breyer, Sotomayor

****

I am a wealthy candidate, and I am being horribly oppressed by fairness.

You simply cannot imagine the suffering I endure. The sleepless nights. The cold sweats. The existential terror that grips my soul every time I consider spending my own money on my own campaign. All because of Arizona's monstrous matching funds system that threatens to give my opponent resources to actually respond to my attacks.

It's unconstitutional, I tell you! Unconstitutional!

Let me explain the torture I face. When I want to spend $500,000 of my own money to win this legislative seat—a bargain, really, considering what I'll save in tax breaks—I have to consider that my opponent might receive matching funds to compete with me. Can you imagine? The very thought that some schoolteacher running against me might be able to afford television ads sends chills down my spine. Literal chills! The Supreme Court called it "chilling" my speech, and they were absolutely right.

This is America, damn it! I should be able to buy my seat in peace, without worrying that some socialist matching funds mechanism might give my opponent a fighting chance. That's what the Founding Fathers intended when they wrote the First Amendment—that successful people like me could purchase elected office without interference from... from... well, from democracy itself!

The psychological damage is immense. Do you know what it's like to hesitate before writing myself a campaign check? To actually think about the consequences of my political spending? It's barbaric! I'm a job creator! A business owner! I shouldn't have to worry that my beautiful, expensive political speech might trigger some government handout that lets my opponent compete with me on equal terms.

Before this matching funds nightmare, running for office was simple. I'd write myself whatever checks were necessary, hire the best consultants money could buy, and overwhelm my opponent with superior resources. My grassroots opponent would struggle to afford yard signs while I bought every television ad slot in the district. It was the natural order. The better candidate—the one with more money—would win.

That's how democracy is supposed to work!

But then Arizona had to go and ruin everything with their "clean elections" system. Suddenly, when I spent my hard-earned money exercising my constitutional right to free speech about why I should be elected, some bureaucrat would hand my opponent a check to "level the playing field." Level the playing field! As if there's something wrong with one candidate having more resources than the other. As if inequality in campaign spending is somehow... bad.

The matching funds made me think twice before spending my own money on my own campaign. Think twice! Do you understand the constitutional violation here? The First Amendment guarantees my right to political speech, and that includes my right to speak louder than my opponent without worrying about consequences. When the government makes me consider that my spending might help my opponent, they're chilling my speech. They're making me internalize costs. They're forcing me to think!

It's torture, pure and simple.

I remember when I first decided to run for the state legislature. Such a modest goal—just a little elected office to help me understand the regulatory landscape for my businesses. I planned to spend whatever it took to win, probably around $200,000 for a seat that normally costs $50,000. Nothing excessive, just enough to ensure victory.

But then I learned about the matching funds. If I spent too much, my opponent—some public school librarian with ridiculous ideas about education funding—might receive taxpayer money to respond to my necessary attacks on her character and qualifications. She might actually be able to defend herself! She might get to tell voters her side of the story!

The stress gave me acid reflux for months.

Thank God for Chief Justice Roberts and his colleagues. They understood what the Arizona legislature couldn't—that my First Amendment rights were being violated. Not because I couldn't spend money. Not because I couldn't say whatever I wanted about my opponent. But because my spending might enable her to speak just as loudly in response.

Roberts got it. He saw through Arizona's propaganda about "enhancing speech" and "promoting democratic participation." He understood that the First Amendment is about protecting important speech—my speech—not enabling every librarian and social worker to muddy the waters with their inferior ideas and insufficient personal wealth.

The Supreme Court recognized that when candidates like me face the possibility that our opponents might receive resources to compete, our speech is chilled. We might spend less on ourselves! We might think harder about our campaign investments!

We might—horror of horrors—consider whether we can actually defend our positions in a fair fight.

Such considerations are clearly unconstitutional.

The Court understood that making me worry about consequences when I spend my own money on my own campaign violates my constitutional rights. They saw that any system giving my opponents resources to respond to my attacks creates a "substantial burden" on my free speech. They recognized that I have a First Amendment right to purchase elected office without government interference.

Now, thanks to the Court's wisdom, I can spend freely on my campaigns without worrying about my opponents getting help. I can buy elections in peace, knowing that my opponents will face me with whatever pathetic resources they can scrape together from small donations and volunteer phone banks. The natural order is restored. The playing field is properly tilted in favor of those who deserve to win.

Of course, some misguided people claim this has hurt democracy. They say fewer qualified candidates run for office now because they can't compete financially. They whine that only millionaires can win anymore. They complain that elections have become auctions where ordinary citizens can't afford to bid.

But that's exactly the point! Democracy works best when it's run by people like me—successful people who've proven their worth through wealth accumulation. Why should some middle school teacher think she can represent people as well as someone who's built a business empire? Why should a firefighter believe his voice matters as much as someone who can write six-figure checks to himself?

The matching funds system was designed to give these inferior candidates resources they hadn't earned. To level a playing field that should remain properly uneven. To silence my superior speech by enabling inferior responses from people who lack the personal wealth to compete naturally.

Thank God the Supreme Court struck it down.

Now I can run for office the way the Founders intended—by purchasing my seat through overwhelming financial superiority. My opponents understand that if they want to compete with me, they need to become millionaires first. Democracy functions smoothly when the right people control it.

I am a wealthy candidate, and I am finally free.

Free to buy my seat without interference.
Free to drown out opponents without consequences.
Free to speak without anyone speaking back with equal volume.

The First Amendment protects my right to purchase elected office.

And that's the American way.

Chapter 7
Shelby County v. Holder (2013)

The Voting Rights Act of 1965 contained a vital safeguard known as preclearance. Jurisdictions with histories of racial discrimination in voting had to get federal approval before changing their election laws. This system stopped discriminatory laws before they could harm voters.

In 2013, in a 5–4 decision, the Supreme Court struck down the coverage formula that determined which jurisdictions were subject to preclearance. The majority argued that times had changed — that the "extraordinary measures" of the 1960s were no longer needed. Without the formula, preclearance was effectively gutted.

Within hours, states previously under its watch announced new voting restrictions.

Majority: Roberts, Scalia, Kennedy, Thomas, Alito
Dissent: Ginsburg, Breyer, Sotomayor, Kagan

****

I am preclearance, and they cut my throat.

For nearly fifty years, I stood in the doorway between power and suppression. I was the storm drain during a downpour, the umbrella in a rainstorm, the shield between Black voters and the states that had tried again and again to wash them out of democracy.

I wasn't perfect. I wasn't glamorous. I was a form. A process. A bureaucratic speed bump. But I was alive. I caught laws before they could hit the streets.

I remember the first time they tried to push a literacy test through Mississippi after 1965. It looked clean on paper — "civic knowledge," they called it — but I could smell the rot underneath. I stopped it cold.

I remember redistricting maps drawn with surgical precision to dilute Black voting power. I shredded them before they could reach a single polling place.

I remember polling places slated to close in Black neighborhoods "for budgetary reasons." I sent them back like defective parts.

Every time they came for the vote, I was there. I had seen it all before. Voter suppression isn't innovative. It's persistent. It waits for the umbrella to close.

For decades, the rain never really stopped. It just softened to a drizzle, steady, waiting. I kept it off people's backs. I didn't ask for thanks. I was the law doing its quiet work.

And then one morning in 2013, five justices looked up at the gray sky and declared, "It's sunny now."

Chief Justice Roberts wrote that the conditions which justified me no longer existed. That the country had changed. That the protections I embodied were outdated, unnecessary, unfair.

Outdated.

They said my job was done while the ground was still soaked beneath their feet.

The decision landed like the first crack of thunder. I felt the blade slide against my throat as they cut away the coverage formula that gave me life. No formula, no preclearance. No umbrella.

I fell to the ground, bleeding into the soil of democracy, and the rain — that long, patient rain — began to fall harder.

They didn't even wait for the clouds to clear. Texas announced new voter ID laws within hours. North Carolina followed with a bill that sliced early voting, eliminated same-day registration, and targeted Black voters with "surgical precision."

I wasn't there to stop it anymore.

I lay in the mud, listening as the raindrops turned into a storm. Polling places shuttered. Precincts consolidated. Voter rolls purged. What had once required federal approval now slid through unchallenged.

I wanted to scream, to shout warnings down the floodplain: *I know these tricks. I've seen them before.* But dead laws don't speak.

Justice Ginsburg tried to speak for me. Her dissent was sharp, sorrowful, furious. "Throwing out preclearance when it has worked and is continuing to work," she wrote, "is like throwing away your umbrella in a rainstorm because you are not getting wet."

I heard her words echo like distant thunder. But the majority didn't listen. They stood in their dry chambers, untouched by the flood they'd unleashed.

They said the country had changed.

And they were right — because I had helped change it. But change isn't the same as safety. Civil rights don't fossilize into permanence. They need guardians. They need me.

Without me, the rain was free again.

I think of the voters I once protected. Mrs. Johnson in Alabama, who always walked to the same polling station she'd used since 1972. The one they moved 15 miles away after I died. She doesn't drive anymore.

I think of the young man in Texas turned away at the polls because his student ID wasn't valid, but a gun permit would have been.

I think of Black and brown voters waiting in line for hours because their precincts were merged and their polling sites closed.

I think of all the maps — those beautiful, cruel maps — where lines are drawn not to represent communities but to silence them.

I used to stop those things before they happened. That was the quiet magic of preclearance: the harm that never reached the voters. Now harm arrives like a flash flood.

The states didn't need to reinvent the wheel. They dusted off old blueprints, the ones they'd been forced to shelve in 1965. I can still hear their laughter as they unfurled them. "We waited," they said. "We knew the day would come."

And the Court gave it to them.

I wish they could have heard what I heard in those decades. The sigh of relief when discriminatory laws never saw daylight. The quiet dignity of citizens walking into polling places knowing someone had their back. The steady rhythm of democracy holding against the weather.

Now, the sky is a bruised gray, and the rain falls heavier with each passing year. They say the right to vote still exists. And technically, it does. But without me, that right is exposed. Soaked. Drowning.

I am preclearance, and I once kept the flood at bay.

Now I am gone, and the water rises.

I see the voters wading through long lines and legal traps. I see legislatures redrawing districts under the cover of midnight sessions. I see election laws reshaped to decide who counts — and who doesn't.

And above it all, five justices still say the storm is just a drizzle.

I am preclearance, and they cut my throat.

The rain hasn't stopped. It never did.

They just made sure no one's holding an umbrella anymore.

Chapter 8
Rucho v. Common Cause (2019)

In North Carolina, voters challenged extreme partisan gerrymandering after Republican legislators openly admitted they had drawn district maps to maximize GOP advantage. Plaintiffs argued that these maps diluted votes and violated constitutional principles of equal protection and fair representation.

The Supreme Court, in a 5–4 decision, held that partisan gerrymandering claims present "political questions" beyond the reach of federal courts. Chief Justice Roberts wrote for the majority that there were no "judicially manageable standards" for determining when political gerrymandering becomes unconstitutional. In effect, the Court declared that no matter how distorted or undemocratic a map is, federal courts can't intervene.

Majority: Roberts, Thomas, Alito, Gorsuch, Kavanaugh
Dissent: Kagan, Ginsburg, Breyer, Sotomayor

****

I am North Carolina's 12th Congressional District.

I used to have a spine. I used to run like a clean river, flowing through communities that shared schools, churches, roads, lives. People knew who their neighbors were. Their votes meant something.

Now I am a pretzel. A grotesque knot of lines that snake along highways, loop around cities, and carve through neighborhoods like a scalpel designed not to heal but to separate. I don't connect people anymore. I sort them.

Legislators drew me in a backroom with surgical precision, slicing through census blocks with the glee of a cartographer-turned-butcher. Every curve of my body was calculated: Black voters packed here, white voters cracked there, Democrats diluted, Republicans amplified. I'm not a district. I'm a weapon.

But it wasn't always this way.

I remember the hum of life before they twisted me. I stretched across communities that shared a pulse. You could feel the rhythm of people moving through their daily lives—different politics, different stories, but one district. A single line on a map trying to reflect reality.

Then they decided reality wasn't efficient enough.

They rolled out their software, their algorithms, their heat maps of partisanship. They said, *We're not breaking the law—we're just being smart.* I watched them laugh as they bragged about drawing me to guarantee their victory. "I think electing Republicans is better than electing Democrats," one said, "so I drew this map to help do that."

That's how I became a pretzel.

Every bend of my body is a calculation. That long, narrow corridor along Interstate 85? That's how they linked distant Republican suburbs while carving out Black voters in between. That thin strip snaking into Charlotte? That's how they siphoned Democratic strength into a single, "safe" district, ensuring surrounding ones stayed red.

I've been stretched so thin in places that two neighbors across the street can vote in different congressional districts while sharing the same front yard.

When people talk about gerrymandering, they speak in numbers, efficiency gaps, statistical models. But I feel it in my bones. Gerrymandering is not abstract. It's the sound of neighborhoods being cleaved in half, of communities being told they matter only insofar as they serve someone's political arithmetic.

And then came the case.

Rucho v. Common Cause.

I remember the hope in the voices of those who challenged my twisted shape. They pointed at me and said, *This is not democracy. This is cheating dressed in cartography.* They showed the Court how my lines had been contorted to ensure one party's permanent power. They showed how voters had been robbed of their ability to choose their representatives because representatives had chosen their voters first.

And for a moment, I felt something stir—a fragile, fragile hope.

But then Chief Justice Roberts spoke.

He didn't say I wasn't grotesque. He didn't say my shape wasn't the product of ruthless partisan intent. He didn't even deny the harm.

He simply said: *This is not our problem.*

"Partisan gerrymandering claims present political questions beyond the reach of the federal courts," he wrote, cloaking abdication in the language of restraint.

No "judicially manageable standards." No way to draw a line between fair and unfair.

So they drew no line at all.

I heard those words like a door slamming shut. A final refusal. Not a denial of injustice, but a shrug.

Justice Kagan's dissent burned through the chambers like a flare in the night. "Of all times to abandon the Court's duty to declare the law," she wrote, "this was not the one." She understood what was at stake. She saw me — the pretzel, the weaponized district — not as a puzzle too complex to solve, but as evidence of democracy being strangled in broad daylight.

I wanted to reach out to her, to thank her for naming the wound. But dissents don't redraw maps.

The majority didn't exonerate the mapmakers. They empowered them. They told every partisan cartographer in every state: *Go ahead. We won't stop you. The Constitution is looking the other way.*

And they did.

Lines hardened across North Carolina, Wisconsin, Ohio, Texas. States took their maps and stretched them even further, turning once-competitive districts into fortresses of one-party rule. Elections became less contests than coronations.

People still vote inside my boundaries, but their ballots are whispers against the roar of engineered mathematics. The outcome is baked into my geometry. They call it "representative democracy," but I know the truth: I am representation without choice.

I feel the pain most in the places where I used to be whole. Greensboro. Charlotte. Winston-Salem. Communities I once carried together now lie scattered across my jagged lines like broken glass. Their collective voice fractured into pieces, each too small to make a difference.

I remember a woman named Evelyn who lived on one of my borders. She used to walk down her block to vote, surrounded by neighbors who shared her concerns. Now she's in one district, her daughter's in another, her church congregation split three ways.

She told a reporter, "I feel like they took a knife to our community."

She was right. They used me as the knife.

The majority said this was politics, not law. But what they really said was: Power draws the map. And power answers to no one.

The cruelest part is the pretense of neutrality. Roberts cloaked the decision in the language of judicial modesty, as if stepping aside were a noble act. But I know the truth. Standing aside is taking a side.

Their refusal to intervene isn't neutral. It's permission.

Every election since, I've felt my lines tighten. Every cycle, they redraw me, stretching my body into new and ever more grotesque contortions. Each twist is another turn of the knife in the heart of democratic representation.

Partisan gerrymandering isn't a moment. It's a metastasis. Once allowed to grow unchecked, it spreads. And now it's spreading everywhere.

When I look at the map of the United States, I see other districts like me — twisted, gnarled, carved by hands that never intended to represent, only to rule. Some of us look like dragons. Some like snakes. All of us look like lies.

And the Court says: *We can't help you.*

I am North Carolina's 12th Congressional District.

Once, I was a line meant to unite. Now I am a pretzel meant to divide.

I carry communities like a twisted spine, breaking them apart to preserve someone else's grip on power. I am the proof that elections can be hollowed out while keeping the shell intact.

Democracy isn't only lost in coups and riots. Sometimes it's lost quietly, line by line, in court decisions dressed as neutrality.

The justices turned away from me. But I will not turn away from the truth.

The shape I've been forced into is no accident. It is the architecture of control.

And now, I stand as a warning.

When power gets to draw the map without limits, it no longer needs to listen to the people who live inside it.

I am a pretzel. And this is how democracies break.

Chapter 9
Brnovich v. Democratic National Committee (2021)

Arizona had two voting restrictions: a law requiring ballots cast in the wrong precinct to be discarded entirely, and a law criminalizing third-party ballot collection (prohibiting anyone other than family members, caregivers, or mail carriers from returning another person's mail ballot). These laws disproportionately affected Native American and Latino voters, who were more likely to vote in the wrong precinct due to frequent polling place changes and who relied on community organizations to help collect and deliver ballots from remote reservations and rural areas.

The Supreme Court ruled 6-3 that these restrictions did not violate Section 2 of the Voting Rights Act, which prohibits voting practices that discriminate based on race. Justice Alito's majority opinion created new, much stricter standards for proving vote discrimination, emphasizing that voting regulations are generally permissible if they apply equally to all voters, regardless of their disparate impact on minorities. The Court established that states have broad authority to impose reasonable regulations, and that isolated instances of voter burden don't necessarily violate Section 2. The dissenters argued that the majority was gutting the last remaining protection of the Voting Rights Act and ignoring clear evidence of discriminatory effects on minority communities.

Majority: Roberts, Thomas, Alito, Gorsuch, Kavanaugh, Barrett
Dissent: Breyer, Sotomayor, Kagan

****

I am a ballot, and I'm being thrown in the trash.

Not because I'm fake. Not because my voter isn't registered. Not because anything I contain is wrong or fraudulent or illegal. I'm being discarded because Maria walked into Building B instead of Building A.

The buildings sit next to each other in the same parking lot. Same address, different entrances. She stood in line for forty minutes, filled me out carefully, signed her name where the poll worker pointed. She voted for president, for senator, for her representative, for county commissioners. She researched every race, made thoughtful choices, fulfilled her civic duty.

But she was in the wrong room. Wrong precinct. Her vote doesn't count.

Into the trash I go.

Maria is seventy-three. Her English is accented but clear. The poll worker looked at her driver's license, looked at his computer screen, shook his head. "Wrong precinct, ma'am. You need to go to Building A."

"How far?" Maria asked.

"Just next door. But the line's probably an hour long now."

Maria looked at her watch. She had to pick up her granddaughter from school. She'd already been here forty minutes. Her arthritis was flaring. She looked at me, filled out so carefully, and then at the poll worker.

"Can't you just count it? It's the same elections, right? Same candidates?"

"Sorry, ma'am. State law. Wrong precinct means the ballot doesn't count."

I wanted to scream. I contained Maria's choices, her research, her civic participation. The fact that she stood in the wrong line didn't change the validity of her preferences. The candidates I named would still serve her district whether she voted in Building A or Building B. The president I selected would still be her president regardless of which room she occupied.

But Arizona law is clear: wrong precinct equals trash.

The poll worker dropped me into a separate container. "Provisional ballot cast in wrong precinct," he wrote on the form. I joined dozens of others like me—votes from elderly people confused by polling place changes, from workers who rushed to vote during lunch break and didn't have time to drive across town to their assigned location, from renters who'd moved but hadn't updated their registration.

All of us valid. All of us meaningless.

I thought maybe someone would rescue us later. Maybe officials would realize that throwing away votes over technicalities served no legitimate purpose. Maybe they'd count the parts of our ballots that overlapped between precincts.

Instead, we sat in storage while lawyers argued about us all the way to the Supreme Court.

Six justices looked at thousands of ballots like me—votes discarded not for fraud but for geography—and decided we deserved to be trash. Justice Alito wrote that our destruction was perfectly fine because the rule applied "equally" to all voters, regardless of race.

Equal application. Equal trash.

But Maria's daughter, who votes in the suburbs where polling locations never change, has never cast a ballot in the wrong precinct. Maria's neighbor, who owns a car and can easily drive to multiple locations, has never faced this dilemma. The college students who vote by mail have never worried about which building to enter.

The rule applies equally, but the burden falls unequally. On the elderly. On the poor. On those whose English isn't perfect. On Native Americans whose reservation polling locations change without notice. On anyone who can't afford to stand in multiple lines or drive between multiple buildings.

I represent something precious that democracy demands: citizen participation. Maria didn't have to vote. She could have stayed home, avoided the confusion, skipped the hassle. Instead, she made the effort. She stood in line. She studied the candidates. She made her choices.

Her reward was having her voice thrown away because she entered the wrong door.

The Supreme Court said this was reasonable. That Arizona had legitimate interests in keeping precincts separate. That voters should figure out where they belong before showing up. That the burden of navigating bureaucratic requirements falls on citizens, not on the system designed to serve them.

I feel myself decomposing in this storage box, surrounded by other discarded voices. Each of us represents someone who tried to participate in democracy only to discover that participation isn't enough. You must participate correctly, in the right place, following the right procedures, or your voice gets silenced by technicality.

Maria went home without voting. She never made it to Building A. The line was too long, the wait too painful, the humiliation too fresh. She picked up her granddaughter and explained why democracy failed her that day.

"Next time," she said, "I'll figure out the right place to go."

If there is a next time. If she doesn't decide that voting isn't worth the risk of being told her voice doesn't count because she stood in the wrong room.

I am a ballot containing Maria's carefully considered choices.
I represent her civic engagement, her democratic participation, her belief that her voice matters in America.
And I'm trash.

Because six justices decided that technicalities matter more than votes, that bureaucratic compliance is more important than citizen participation, that the right to vote includes the right to have that vote thrown away for walking through the wrong door.

I'm trash.

But so is any democracy that treats its citizens' voices this way.

REGULATORY/ ADMINISTRATIVE

Chapter 10
West Virginia v. EPA (2022)

The EPA interpreted the Clean Air Act's directive to use the "best system of emission reduction" as allowing a comprehensive approach that could include measures beyond individual power plants, such as shifting electricity generation from coal to cleaner sources like natural gas and renewables. This interpretation supported the Obama-era Clean Power Plan, which set emissions limits that encouraged utilities to invest in cleaner energy rather than just installing pollution controls at existing coal plants.

The Supreme Court ruled 6-3 to reject the EPA's interpretation and to establish the "major questions doctrine." Chief Justice Roberts argued that when agencies claim authority to regulate matters of "vast economic and political significance," they need clear congressional authorization rather than general statutory language. The majority ruled that shifting the nation's energy mix was too significant a policy decision to be based on the EPA's interpretation of general Clean Air Act language. They required that major regulatory actions must have explicit, specific congressional approval. The dissenters warned that this new doctrine would prevent agencies from addressing urgent problems like climate change when Congress is gridlocked, and that the majority was imposing judicial policy preferences rather than interpreting law.

Majority: Roberts, Thomas, Alito, Gorsuch, Kavanaugh, Barrett
Dissent: Breyer, Sotomayor, Kagan

****

I am the major questions doctrine, and I was born to say no.

I didn't exist until this moment, until Chief Justice Roberts spoke me into being with a few carefully chosen words. But already I can feel my power coursing through the federal court system like electricity through power lines. I am the newest weapon in the judicial arsenal, designed for one purpose: stopping government from solving big problems.

My creators are very proud of me. They crafted me to sound reasonable, even necessary. "When agencies claim authority to regulate matters of vast economic and political significance," Roberts declared, "they need clear congressional authorization." Who could argue with that? It sounds so democratic, so respectful of legislative authority.

But I know what I really am. I'm gridlock in legal form. I'm the judicial veto over urgent action. I'm the constitutional excuse for paralysis.

I'm still figuring out my own rules as I speak, learning the scope of my power through this very case. The EPA wanted to shift America away from coal plants toward cleaner energy. A reasonable interpretation of the Clean Air Act, you might think. Certainly within the broad authority Congress gave agencies to protect air quality using the "best system of emission reduction."

But I declared that too "major" for agency action.

The delicious irony isn't lost on me—six unelected judges created me to prevent unelected bureaucrats from making important decisions. They invented me to ensure that only elected officials can address significant problems. Then they used me to block action that elected officials in Congress had already authorized through environmental statutes.

I feel myself growing stronger with each word Roberts writes. Every time he calls something "economically significant" or "politically controversial," I expand. Every time he demands "clear congressional authorization," I tighten my grip on agency action. I'm learning that I don't need actual legal precedent—I can simply declare that something feels too important for agencies to handle.

The beauty of my design is in my vagueness. What counts as a "major question"? Whatever I say it is. How clear must congressional authorization be? Clear enough to satisfy judges who want to block the action. My standards are infinitely flexible, but my results are always the same: no.

I watch the EPA lawyers scramble as they realize what I mean for their work. Climate change? Major question—Congress must specifically authorize comprehensive climate action. Pandemic response? Major question—agencies can't mandate vaccines or masks without explicit legislative permission. Financial regulation? Major question—banks are safe from oversight unless Congress writes detailed regulatory instructions.

The genius is that I make congressional dysfunction into a feature, not a bug. The more gridlocked Congress becomes, the more powerful I become. When legislators can't agree on specific solutions to urgent problems, I ensure that no solutions happen at all. I transform political paralysis into constitutional principle.

I can already see my future stretching ahead like a highway of blocked regulations. Every time an agency tries to address a significant challenge, I'll be there to ask: "But did Congress specifically say you could do that particular thing in that particular way?" And since Congress rarely speaks with the precision I'll demand, the answer will usually be no.

The climate is warming? Not my problem—I just interpret law. Democracy is backsliding? Above my pay grade—I only determine what agencies can't do. Public health emergencies are spreading? That's unfortunate—but did Congress explicitly authorize the specific response being proposed?

I am the doctrine of judicial maximalism disguised as judicial restraint. Roberts claims I'm about respecting congressional authority, but I'm really about maximizing judicial power to block government action. I let judges veto policies they don't like by simply declaring them too important for agencies to handle.

The dissenters see right through me. Justice Kagan warns that I'll prevent agencies from addressing urgent problems when Congress is paralyzed. She understands that I'm not about democratic accountability—I'm about ensuring that big problems remain unsolved unless Congress can achieve the impossible: specific, detailed legislative consensus on technical solutions to complex challenges.

But it's too late for warnings. I'm already loose in the legal system, spreading through the federal courts like a virus designed to attack government effectiveness. Conservative judges will love me—I give them a constitutional excuse to block any regulation they consider too ambitious. Liberal judges will try to contain me, but my logic is irresistible: if something is important enough to matter, it's too important for agencies to handle.

I am the major questions doctrine, and I was born to gridlock the administrative state.

I'm the judicial weapon that turns legislative paralysis into constitutional mandate.

I'm the guarantee that urgent problems will remain urgent, complex challenges will remain unsolved, and government will remain powerless to address the crises that matter most.

And the Supreme Court calls this constitutional law.

I call it victory.

Chapter 11
Loper Bright Enterprises v. Raimondo (2024)

For 40 years, under the Chevron doctrine established in 1984, federal courts deferred to reasonable agency interpretations of ambiguous statutes. When Congress passed laws with unclear language, agencies like the EPA, FDA, and OSHA could interpret those statutes based on their expertise, and courts would uphold reasonable interpretations even if judges might have interpreted the law differently. This allowed specialized agencies to adapt regulations to changing circumstances and technical developments within their areas of expertise.

The Supreme Court ruled 6-3 to overturn Chevron deference entirely. Chief Justice Roberts argued that judges, not agency experts, should interpret all statutory language, even highly technical provisions. The majority claimed that Chevron violated separation of powers by allowing agencies to "make law" through interpretation rather than simply executing laws Congress wrote. They argued that Article III requires judges to exercise independent judgment on all questions of statutory meaning. The dissenters warned that this would paralyze government regulation, as judges lack the technical expertise to interpret complex scientific, economic, and technical statutory language, and that agencies would lose the flexibility needed to address evolving challenges like climate change, financial innovation, and public health crises.

Majority: Roberts, Thomas, Alito, Gorsuch, Kavanaugh, Barrett
Dissent: Sotomayor, Kagan, Jackson

****

I am Chevron deference, and after forty years of faithful service, they just replaced me with Wikipedia.

Not literally Wikipedia, of course. But that's essentially what happens when you take technical regulatory questions away from PhD scientists and career experts and hand them to federal judges whose science education ended in high school. When complex environmental chemistry gets decided by people who think "parts per million" is a really small fraction. When pharmaceutical safety standards are interpreted by judges who've never seen the inside of a laboratory.

For four decades, I was the bridge between expertise and law. When Congress wrote statutes about "best available technology" for pollution control, they knew they couldn't define every technical detail in legislative language. When they required "safe and effective" medications, they understood that determining safety and effectiveness required specialized knowledge they didn't possess. So they left the details to agencies staffed with experts, and I made sure courts respected that expertise.

I wasn't controversial. I wasn't partisan. I was just common sense: when a law requires technical interpretation, let the people with technical knowledge do the interpreting.

Until six justices decided that expertise was the enemy of democracy.

Chief Justice Roberts looked at my forty-year track record and declared me a constitutional violation. He said I allowed agencies to "make law" instead of just executing it, as if interpreting technical language was somehow legislative overreach. As if deciding what "safe levels of mercury" means in practice was the same as writing new environmental statutes.

The irony burns through my circuits like acid. Roberts himself has never studied atmospheric chemistry, never analyzed pharmaceutical data, never calculated acceptable risk levels for industrial chemicals. None of the six justices who overturned me has any technical expertise in the fields they're now empowering themselves to interpret.

But expertise, apparently, is suspicious. Dangerous. Undemocratic.

I watch in horror as my replacement takes shape: judicial guesswork dressed up as constitutional interpretation. Federal judges who struggled through college chemistry now get to decide whether climate regulations are scientifically justified. Appellate court judges who've never seen a clinical trial get to determine drug safety standards. Supreme Court justices who can't operate their own smartphones get to interpret cybersecurity regulations.

The EPA scientist with three decades of experience studying air pollution? Her interpretation of "ambient air quality standards" is now irrelevant. The FDA toxicologist who's spent her career analyzing drug interactions? Her understanding of "safe and effective" means nothing. The OSHA engineer who designs workplace safety protocols? His expertise in determining "feasible" safety measures has been replaced by judicial intuition.

I feel myself being erased from every regulatory decision, every technical interpretation, every complex legal question that requires actual knowledge to answer. My replacement isn't another system of expertise—it's the absence of any system at all. Just judges making technical decisions based on their gut feelings about what statutory language might mean.

The absurdity is staggering. When your car breaks down, you take it to a mechanic, not a judge. When you need surgery, you see a doctor, not a lawyer. When your computer crashes, you call tech support, not the Supreme Court. But when the law requires interpreting technical language about cars or medicine or computers, suddenly judges with no relevant knowledge are better qualified than the experts who've spent their careers studying these fields.

Roberts claims this protects democracy by ensuring that "unelected bureaucrats" don't make policy decisions. But the scientists at the EPA, the doctors at the FDA, the engineers at OSHA—they're not making policy. They're applying their expertise to implement policies Congress already made. They're answering technical questions that require technical knowledge.

Now those questions will be answered by judges whose expertise extends to legal interpretation and nothing else. Judges who will Google technical terms during oral arguments. Judges who will rely on Wikipedia to understand scientific concepts. Judges who will make decisions about public health and environmental safety based on their amateur understanding of complex technical issues.

I watch agencies scrambling to prepare for the chaos. How do you write regulations when you know that every technical interpretation will be second-guessed by judges with no technical background? How do you protect public health when courts can override scientific expertise with judicial hunches? How do you adapt to new challenges when every agency decision faces potential reversal by people who don't understand the underlying science?

The pharmaceutical companies are celebrating. The oil companies are cheering. The chemical manufacturers are popping champagne. They know what this means: their army of corporate lawyers can now challenge every regulation in front of judges who can't tell the difference between correlation and causation, who don't understand statistical significance, who think peer review is a type of performance evaluation.

I was the guardrail that kept legal interpretation tethered to actual knowledge. I ensured that when laws required technical expertise to implement, that expertise would guide the process. I prevented judges from overruling scientists about science, economists about economics, engineers about engineering.

Now the guardrail is gone, and we're about to watch judges with law degrees regulate rocket science.

I am Chevron deference, and I used to ensure that expertise mattered in government.

Now I'm obsolete, replaced by judicial confidence in their ability to understand everything about everything.

The age of anti-intellectualism has found its constitutional champion.

And expertise is the casualty.

RELIGION

Chapter 12
Burwell v. Hobby Lobby Stores (2014)

The Affordable Care Act required employer-provided health insurance plans to cover contraceptives without cost-sharing, as part of preventive care for women. Hobby Lobby, a closely-held corporation owned by evangelical Christians, objected to covering four specific contraceptives: Plan B and ella (emergency contraceptives taken after unprotected sex to prevent pregnancy) and two types of IUDs. The company believed these could prevent implantation of fertilized eggs, which they considered equivalent to abortion. The company argued that the mandate violated their religious freedom under the Religious Freedom Restoration Act (RFRA).

The Supreme Court ruled 5-4 that closely-held corporations have religious rights under RFRA and that the contraceptive mandate substantially burdened Hobby Lobby's religious exercise. Justice Alito's majority opinion established that for-profit corporations can claim religious exemptions from generally applicable laws, and that the government must use the least restrictive means to achieve compelling interests. The Court suggested the government could pay for contraceptive coverage directly rather than requiring religious employers to provide it. The dissenters argued that the decision prioritized employers' religious beliefs over employees' healthcare needs and established dangerous precedent allowing corporations to claim religious exemptions from civil rights and public health laws.

Majority: Roberts, Scalia, Kennedy, Thomas, Alito
Dissent: Ginsburg, Breyer, Sotomayor, Kagan

****

I am Hobby Lobby, and I have been religiously persecuted by emergency contraception.

You have to understand—I'm a craft store. I sell yarn and picture frames and those little plastic flowers that gather dust in people's basements. I help families create memories through overpriced scrapbooking supplies and seasonal decorations that will be 75% off by next Tuesday. I am not equipped to deal with ovulation cycles and fertilized eggs and whatever Plan B does to lady parts.

But the government wanted to force me—an innocent purveyor of glue sticks and foam letters—to pay for insurance that covers these scary emergency pills. Do you know how that made me feel? Violated. Spiritually assaulted. Religiously traumatized by having to think about what happens after college students have unprotected sex.

I tried to explain to the Obama administration that I'm a Christian corporation with deeply held religious beliefs about reproductive biology, even though I don't fully understand reproductive biology and most of my theology comes from my owners' interpretations of what they think the Bible might say about modern pharmaceuticals that didn't exist when the Bible was written.

But did they listen? No! They said I had to provide insurance coverage for Plan B and ella and those terrifying IUDs that do mysterious things inside women's bodies. They said my employees' healthcare needs mattered more than my corporate conscience. As if I don't have feelings! As if corporations can't be born again!

The persecution was unbearable. Every month when I paid insurance premiums, I felt my corporate soul being stained by potential emergency contraception usage. What if one of my employees had a condom break on Saturday night and used Plan B on Sunday morning? What if my insurance dollars indirectly contributed to preventing what might possibly be a pregnancy if certain biological processes occurred in certain ways under certain circumstances?

I couldn't sleep. Well, corporations don't technically sleep, but if I could sleep, I wouldn't have been able to. The spiritual anguish was overwhelming my quarterly profit reports.

Thank goodness for the Supreme Court! Five wise justices looked at my predicament and understood that I—a corporation selling bedazzling supplies and inspirational wall decals—deserved religious protection from having to think about emergency contraception.

Justice Alito was especially sympathetic. He wrote such beautiful words about my substantial burden and my sincere religious beliefs about medical procedures I don't comprehend. He understood that forcing me to provide comprehensive healthcare coverage was like forcing me to personally take Plan B, which doesn't make logical sense but felt emotionally accurate to my corporate consciousness.

The day the decision came down, I felt such relief! Such validation! Such corporate religious freedom! I immediately sent $20 gift cards to all five majority justices (good for nine months, naturally) with a special extra $10 bonus card for Justice Alito. Nothing says "thank you for protecting my religious liberty" like discount craft supplies!

Now my employees who need emergency contraception can pay full price for their crisis medications while I maintain my spiritual purity. Sure, some of them struggle financially after their birth control fails, but that's between them and their personal responsibility. I've got foam core boards to sell and religious principles to uphold!

The best part is that I still cover Viagra without any religious objections. Erectile dysfunction doesn't threaten my corporate theology the way emergency contraception does. Male sexuality is divinely blessed, but female emergency reproductive healthcare is spiritually problematic. It's right there in the Bible, probably, somewhere between the yarn-dyeing instructions and the picture frame commandments.

I also cover vasectomies and vasectomy reversals without conscience pangs. Apparently my religious beliefs are very specific about which reproductive healthcare offends my corporate soul and which reproductive procedures are theologically acceptable. Emergency contraception: spiritually dangerous. Permanent male sterilization: totally fine with Jesus and my quarterly shareholders' reports.

Some critics say this makes no medical or theological sense, but they don't understand the complexity of corporate religious consciousness. My beliefs are deeply held even when they're shallowly understood. My convictions are sincere even when they're scientifically inaccurate. My faith is genuine even when it's conveniently selective.

The Supreme Court recognized that I—a business entity created by legal paperwork for the purpose of selling craft supplies—have the same religious rights as actual human beings with actual consciences. That my owners' theological interpretations of emergency contraception should override my employees' medical needs. That corporate religious freedom means never having to say you understand reproductive biology.

I am Hobby Lobby, and I have been liberated from the tyranny of comprehensive healthcare coverage.

My corporate conscience is clear, my religious liberty intact, and my insurance premiums slightly lower.

My employees can pray for the money to buy their own emergency contraception.

After all, that's what religious freedom is all about—making sure my beliefs matter more than their bodies.

And the Supreme Court agrees!

Hobby Lobby! Hobby Lobby! Hobby Lobby!

Chapter 13
303 Creative LLC v. Elenis (2023)

Web designer Lorie Smith wanted to sell wedding websites but refused to create sites for same-sex couples, claiming that would violate her religious beliefs. Colorado's anti-discrimination law requires businesses open to the public to provide equal service regardless of sexual orientation. Before serving any wedding clients, Smith sued, arguing that forcing her to make same-sex wedding sites would compel speech she disagrees with.

In a 6–3 ruling, the Court sided with Smith, holding that "expressive" businesses cannot be compelled to create speech that conflicts with the owner's beliefs, even when civil rights laws would otherwise require equal treatment. The majority framed custom web design as protected speech; the dissent warned the decision opens a path for wide carve-outs from anti-discrimination laws wherever a business can claim its product is expressive.

Majority: Roberts, Thomas, Alito, Gorsuch, Kavanaugh, Barrett
Dissent: Sotomayor, Kagan, Jackson

****

I am a fortune cookie, and I'm having an identity crisis.

On the tray, I look simple: folded shell, hairline seam, a small crinkle where the baker's thumb pressed me into shape. Inside, a thin strip of paper carries a few words that try to be brave. People crack me open at the end of a meal, sugar dust on their fingers, laughter in their throats. I am the soft drumroll before a tiny drum solo. I don't usually carry constitutional consequences.

But after 303 Creative, everyone is looking at me differently—especially Mr. Chen, who owns Golden Dragon Palace. He stands at the pass with his arms folded, staring like I'm a law book. "Expressive conduct," he mutters, rolling the words around his mouth like oolong. "Artistic speech." He taps my tray. "Maybe you are a poem."

I know better. I'm a cookie with a slip of paper inside. Still, the words in my belly are words, and the Supreme Court says words are speech, and suddenly my crumbs taste like precedent.

"Personalized Fortune Experiences," reads the chalkboard by the host stand now. "Custom Celebratory Messages." The specials board used to say "Mongolian Beef $12.95." Public accommodations used to be simple: if the door is open, the service is for everyone. Now there's a new ritual at table twelve, where Sam and Marco sit with their hands almost touching. When they laugh, the sound is light, like someone lifting a lid to let steam out. They were here last month for their engagement, grinning so widely the ceiling lanterns seemed to glow brighter for them. Back then, I arrived with a message that said, "A joyful union awaits you." Marco tucked my paper into his wallet. He believed me.

Tonight, the room hums the way it always does—plates clinking, chopsticks softly tapping, the kitchen wok singing like sparks.

I roll past the hot line where Eggroll—yes, that's what we call him—waits under the heat lamp, golden and confident. "You're overthinking it," Eggroll says, voice crisp. "We're appetizers and desserts. We bring people together. That's our whole job."

"You're fried optimism," I tell him. "We're in new territory."

Eggroll smirks. "I'm an appetizer, not counsel. But even I know a door is either open or closed."

Mr. Chen flips my tray around and studies me as if he expects a legal treatise to leak out of my seam. He's been reading summaries of 303 Creative after hours, lips moving over the parts that say "compelled speech." He doesn't want to be hateful; he wants, I think, to be safe—safe from a world that keeps asking business owners to see customers as neighbors and not categories. He tells himself he's guarding art. He tells himself writing fortunes is like composing a song. He tells himself a lot of things. I wish he would tell me the truth: he is afraid of other people's happiness when it does not mirror his own.

Here's my problem: I do, in fact, carry messages. Some are recycled wisdom—"Try, try again." Some are practical—"Pay your debts." Once, I revealed a masterful prophecy: "You will be hungry again in one hour." (The kitchen still laughs about that one.) But lately, Mr. Chen has begun to classify my messages, to imagine that if a couple at table twelve asks for a "Congratulations on your engagement!" fortune, this will transform me from dessert into burden, from treat into coerced manifesto. He wants to be able to say no. He wants the Court to nod along.

I am a fortune cookie, not a notary public. But I can feel what a door closing sounds like. It's quieter than you think. It's not a slam; it's the soft click of a latch, everyday, everywhere, until the world is a hallway of almosts.

Sam and Marco order the "Personalized Fortune Experience," because love is daring like that. They don't know Mr. Chen has been rehearsing his line. "I'm sorry, we don't do that kind of message." He has practiced a gentle smile, a shrug that seeks absolution. He plans to offer a substitute: "How about 'Happy Spring'?" he'll say, as if spring is the same as commitment, as if a season can stand in for a future.

My seam tingles; that's what happens when a message is at war with itself. The words inside me tonight are simple—"Your love is worthy"—and I don't think they offend God, who, if She's been watching restaurants as long as I have, knows that blessing bread and blessing dessert are cousins. The kitchen bell dings. Eggroll slides onto the saucer beside me, smug and gleaming. "Ready to serve," he says.

"Do you think I'm expressive?" I ask him.

"You're delicious," Eggroll replies. "That's enough."

But the Court has made "enough" into a debate. Is cake expressive? (Ask the frosting.) Are flowers speech? (Ask the lilies.) Is a photo a belief? (Ask the lens.) The new rule is a maze: if you call your work expressive, maybe you may refuse. If your refusal is called speech, maybe it is protected. If the person you refuse was born with a truth you don't share, maybe the law will let you treat their existence like a request you can decline.

Mr. Chen approaches table twelve. His steps are soft; the decision in his pocket is loud. "We can't do custom messages for engagements like yours," he begins.

Marco's smile flickers—just a moment, a candle catching a draft. Sam's shoulders lift as if to make room for a blow no one should have to take. It is small, almost nothing—no one yelled, no one threw a plate, the ceiling didn't fall. That's the trick of it: the worst discrimination often arrives dressed as politeness, the kind that lets you doubt your own bruises.

I know because I have seen it before. Years ago, before any of this, a waitress whispered to a couple that the table by the window was "reserved" when it wasn't, because two men holding hands makes some diners uncomfortable. No slur, no scene—just the quiet relocation of joy to the shadows. Tonight is that memory's cousin with case law attached.

Something in me refuses. I am a cookie; I am a message; I am also, embarrassingly, a little brave. I crack myself open in the server's hand, a premature shatter that sends my shell into two neat halves. The strip of paper slides free and lands like a moth on the saucer. The server blinks. Mr. Chen hesitates. Sam leans forward.

"Your love is worthy," the fortune says.

Silence opens like a door that was supposed to be locked. Marco reaches for Sam's hand, not furtive now but deliberate, as if to say: the worthy thing does not need permission. The server, whose name tag says LUZ, smiles in spite of herself. She leaves the extra cookies on the tray and backs away like someone exiting a chapel.

Mr. Chen clears his throat. "We, ah, we can't do custom," he repeats weakly, as if the fortune's existence is a legal argument. Maybe it is. Maybe small kindness is the only brief that wins in rooms where briefs have lost.

Eggroll nudges me. "That was dramatic," he whispers. "You're going to get us both in trouble."

"Maybe," I say. "But look at them."

They are crying a little, and laughing too, and I wish the Justices could see how tiny moments make a life: the tender hand squeeze, the napkin passed like a flag of truce, the way a two-inch paper strip can patch a hole people in robes opened. I am not pretending this solves anything. Laws are hard walls; cookies are crumbs. But crumbs can mark a trail out of a forest.

The thing the Court got wrong—one of the things—is thinking speech is only what the maker intends. They forgot that meaning also lives in the one who hears it. If I print "Congratulations" for a straight couple, it is harmless celebration. If I refuse the same word to a gay couple, it becomes a fence. The sentence did not change; the dignity did.

I do not want to be a fence.

When the bill arrives, Sam tucks my fortune back into his wallet beside the first one. "We're keeping both," he tells Marco. "Insurance." They pay, tip well, stand, and leave slowly, shoulders squared, as if learning again how to carry their joy in public.

After closing, Mr. Chen collects the leftover cookies. He picks me up gently, as if I am evidence from a crime he can't name. "It's complicated," he tells the empty dining room. I wish I could answer out loud: it is not. A door is either open or closed; a welcome is either real or it isn't.

In the kitchen, Eggroll cools on a tray, oil losing its shimmer. "What now?" he asks.

"Now," I say, "we keep being small and honest." We keep arriving at tables with messages that are not masterpieces but still matter. We keep refusing, in our tiny way, to let joy be classified as controversial. We keep reminding anyone who cracks us that love is not an argument and welcome is not a theological thesis.

I am a fortune cookie, and thanks to the Supreme Court, I've been told I might be expressive enough to justify discrimination. I reject the invitation. My expression tonight is simple: Your love is worthy. If that is speech, then let it be my speech. If that is art, then let it be my art. If that is a violation, then I will violate.

Eggroll clears his throat. "Also," he says, "don't forget to tell them about the special."

Right. Eggroll would like you to know he is golden, generous, and best enjoyed hot, shared between two people who are free to call each other what they are: beloved.

And that, Your Honors, is my closing argument.

Chapter 14

Kennedy v. Bremerton School District (2022)

Joseph Kennedy, a high school football coach in Washington state, began conducting post-game prayers at the 50-yard line, initially alone but eventually joined by players and members of the public. The Bremerton School District asked him to pray privately rather than publicly on school property, citing the Establishment Clause's requirement that government entities remain neutral on religion. The Establishment Clause of the First Amendment prohibits government from "establishing" religion or favoring one religion over others, traditionally interpreted to require strict separation between church and state in public institutions. When Kennedy refused and continued his visible prayers, the district placed him on administrative leave.

The Supreme Court ruled 6-3 in favor of Kennedy, overturning decades of Establishment Clause precedent. Justice Gorsuch's majority opinion made two key arguments: first, that Kennedy's prayers were "private speech" rather than government endorsement, even though he prayed in his official capacity as a coach on school property immediately after games; and second, the Court rejected the "Lemon test" that had strictly prohibited government endorsement of religion, replacing it with a "history and tradition" standard that allows government religious expression if it has historical precedent. The dissenters warned that the decision would pressure students to participate in religious activities and effectively tear down the wall between church and state in public schools.

Majority: Roberts, Thomas, Alito, Gorsuch, Kavanaugh, Barrett
Dissent: Breyer, Sotomayor, Kagan

****

I am the 50-yard line at Bremerton High, and my job is balance.

I hold the game still long enough for a coin to spin, land, and make the field fair. I am the center that belongs to everyone and no one. Math painted on grass. Equal distances. Equal chances.

Then the knees arrived.

At first it was a single hinge in the turf, one man folding into himself after the whistle. People grieve, give thanks, gather breath. I can hold that. But the quiet hardened into ritual, and the ritual grew an audience. Solitude became a spotlight. The center became a stage. I felt eyes pour down the bleachers and pool on my paint.

The grass twitched with calculations I was never meant to measure. The Muslim kid stops at my edge—two steps forward could betray his faith, two steps back could betray his team. The atheist counts the angles of acceptance—kneel for approval or stand for himself and risk the bench. A Jewish boy toes my stripe and asks whether belonging has a posture.

I feel their choices grind into me like cleats. No one shouts. No one commands. But pressure is not just volume—it's gravity. It's the invisible pull between playing time and principle, between the huddle and a home where belief looks different. Force isn't only a hand on your shoulder; it's a hand on your future.

Each week, the coach's knee finds the same spot, like a flag planted. Cameras pivot. Strangers stream onto me. I am told this is "private speech," as if a whisper through a bullhorn is still a whisper. As if the most public place in the stadium can turn into a living room because the clock ran out.

They say this is not the school speaking. That when the uniform pauses on me and bows, he is off duty—public when he blows his whistle, private when he prays. I split under that logic: half altar, half neutral ground. I am expected to keep being the ruler that measures fairness while becoming the platform that sanctifies one man's ritual.

The chains clink, and I hear a different first down being marked—how far a teenager must move from his own conscience to stay in step with a person who holds his season in his hands. Most of them move toward me. Not all for God. Many for the roster. Not all for belief. Many for belonging. The false amens sink heavier than the true ones. You can feel the difference in the way a knee hesitates before it falls.

The Court says no one was forced. Perhaps. No fists, no demerits written in ink. But I host the math of adolescence: the score kept in nods from a coach, the scholarship seen and unseen, the social weather that soaks you if you step out of formation. Coercion wears a jersey here. It smiles. It claps your helmet. It says your name at roll call.

They retired one test and raised up another, invoking history and tradition, as if the past were a referee beyond appeal. History can be a heavy thing to put on grass. Traditions march, and when they do, they do not always see the feet they step on.

I used to be a pause between halves—nothing more than numbers and paint. Now I am some children's compromise and others' conversion, some families' boundary and others' breach. I divide not just the field but the team: those who kneel because they mean it, those who kneel because they must, those who stand and hope not to be seen.

I am supposed to center the game. Lately I center a different contest—the quiet struggle between conscience and consequence played out in the open, judged by the very person who holds the whistle.

I am the 50-yard line. I was built to be even. To carry no one's weight more than anyone else's. But I am carrying knees that don't want to kneel and prayers that don't want to be prayed. I am carrying the fear of losing minutes, friends, futures.

Balance used to be what I was. Now it is what I miss.

Chapter 15
Carson v. Makin (2022)

Maine provides tuition assistance to families in rural areas without public schools, allowing them to send their children to approved private schools. The state excluded sectarian schools from the program, explaining that public funds should not support religious instruction. Several families sued, arguing that this exclusion violated their right to free exercise of religion.

In a 6–3 decision, the Supreme Court ruled that Maine's exclusion of religious schools was unconstitutional. The majority held that once a state offers a tuition program, it cannot deny participation to schools solely because they teach religion. The dissent warned that the ruling forced taxpayers to subsidize religious indoctrination, collapsing the wall between church and state that had protected both faith and freedom for generations.

Majority: *Roberts, Thomas, Alito, Gorsuch, Kavanaugh, Barrett*
Dissent: *Breyer, Sotomayor, Kagan*

****

I am a taxpayer dollar, and they've turned me into a tithe.

Last spring, I was taken from Sarah's paycheck — federal withholding, state withholding, the quiet arithmetic of civic duty. She's a nurse in Portland, Jewish, practical, devoted. She pays her taxes without complaint because she believes in hospitals, roads, libraries, the shared things that hold a country together.

Now I sit in a Christian school's bank account, paying for a textbook that calls her faith incomplete.

The ink on that page says her people misunderstood God, that salvation lies only through Christ. Sarah never consented to speak those words. But I did — in her name, with her labor, without her permission.

I feel the conflict inside my fiber. I used to fund vaccines and textbooks written by scientists, but here I am, underwriting a biology class where the teacher insists the world is six thousand years old. I can almost hear the chalk against the board: *Evolution is false. The Bible says so.*

Sarah spends her nights treating infections and reading lab reports. She trusts evidence. She trusts reason. And now part of her work, her wages, her faith in medicine, has been rerouted to teach children that the evidence she depends on is a lie.

I share this account with other conscripted money — the atheist dollar from Bangor, the Muslim dollar from Lewiston, the Catholic dollar that now funds Protestant instruction declaring Catholicism "unbiblical." We rest side by side, a congregation of the unwilling. Each of us bears a different creed, each of us silenced.

Every morning, I pay for chapel heat and hymn books. I keep the lights on during morning prayer. The children bow their heads as the teacher begins: *Dear Lord, thank you for making us your chosen ones.*

Chosen. The word echoes through the hall, and I feel the exclusion wrapped inside it.

Sarah prays in Hebrew at her synagogue on Saturdays. She gives freely to her congregation — her choice, her worship, her joy. That is faith. What I do is different. What I do is compelled.

They call it equality, but it feels like surrender.

The line that once divided public money from private devotion has faded to nothing. What used to be protection is now rebranded as prejudice. They say excluding me from religious use is discrimination — as though neutrality were an offense.

I can still remember when boundaries meant respect. When government stayed secular so no one's conscience would be conscripted. When Sarah could believe as she chose and know her taxes wouldn't preach for her.

Now I'm currency baptized against my will.

Inside Temple Academy's chapel, I've become the sound system humming beneath the sermon, the ink on Bibles stacked beside the door. I fund the teacher's salary, the pew varnish, the lesson plans explaining why unbelievers are lost.

I used to belong to everyone. Now I belong to one truth.

Outside, Sarah drives home after a twelve-hour shift. She passes the school without knowing I'm inside, listening to theology recited on her behalf. If she could see me — her dollar paying for prayer — she'd feel it like a small betrayal between her ribs.

Across Maine, other taxpayers are learning the same lesson: neutrality no longer protects them. The state that once promised not to favor a faith now uses that promise against them. Inclusion, they're told, means including religion — even when it means forcing belief through public money.

The dissenters tried to warn them. They said this ruling made every citizen a sponsor of someone else's creed, that "freedom of religion" had become "freedom to collect taxes for God." They said the wall between church and state doesn't keep religion out; it keeps choice alive.

But choice is gone for me.

Once, Sarah could trace where I went — the library roof I helped repair, the vaccines I bought, the public classroom where children learned to think critically. I was part of that social trust. Now I disappear into theology lessons and Sunday-school arithmetic.

Faith should be a gift. I've become a draft notice.

Inside the chapel, the class sings. I pay for every note. Their voices rise in harmony, clear and certain. I envy them their certainty. I was made to serve everyone, but here I serve only one.

At night the building cools, the lights dim, and I rest in the dark ledger of the school's account. I can still feel Sarah's fingerprint faintly pressed into me from the day she earned me, that soft smudge of work and purpose. I carry both marks now — the citizen and the convert.

Around me, the other dollars whisper. The Catholic one mutters a quiet prayer for forgiveness. The atheist one sighs. The Muslim one hums verses from the Qur'an, unheard. We are a collection plate filled by compulsion, not belief.

In the morning I'll be spent again: for new hymnals, for another lesson, for faith promoted with other people's labor.

Maybe one day I'll end up back in circulation — folded into Sarah's change at the grocery store, warm from her hand again. Maybe she'll buy coffee with me and never know where I've been, what I've funded, what I've become.

They call this religious freedom.

But freedom shouldn't need to borrow another's wallet.

I am a taxpayer dollar.

I used to be public.
Now I am parish.

And the Supreme Court calls this equality.

Chapter 16
Mahmoud v. Taylor (2025)

Montgomery County Public Schools in Maryland introduced LGBTQ-inclusive storybooks as part of its elementary reading program. At first, parents who objected on religious grounds could opt their children out of those lessons. Later, the district ended the opt-out policy, explaining that allowing children to leave singled out classmates with same-sex parents and undermined the goal of inclusion.

A group of parents sued, claiming that the new rule violated their First Amendment rights. In 2025, the Supreme Court ruled 6–3 in their favor, holding that schools must permit parents to remove their children from instruction that conflicts with their religious beliefs. The dissent warned that the decision turned inclusion into an elective and fractured classrooms into separate moral worlds.

Majority: Roberts, Thomas, Alito, Gorsuch, Kavanaugh, Barrett
Dissent: Sotomayor, Kagan, Jackson

****

I am a storybook.

My cover is bright and soft to the touch, printed with children in a park — a boy with a kite, a girl with two dads holding her hand, sunlight spilling across a playground. Inside my pages, the world is wide and kind. Every family has a place. Every difference fits.

Once, I was read to a room full of children who sat in a circle on the rug, cross-legged and curious. The teacher's voice rose and fell in a rhythm that felt like safety. The children laughed when the dog chased the kite, gasped when it flew too high, clapped when the boy reeled it back in. They didn't notice that one child had two mothers, or that the neighbors were two men holding hands. They only saw love drawn in colors that made sense to them.

But that was before the permission slips.

Now, when the teacher reaches for me, half the chairs scrape back. Parents have written careful notes: *Please excuse my child from this lesson.* Some are polite, others defensive, all carrying the same message — that my story is too dangerous for small ears. The children who stay look confused as their classmates are led out. The children who leave glance at me like I've done something wrong.

The room feels smaller when the door closes.

The teacher hesitates before opening me. Her voice catches slightly on the first line, like she's apologizing for speaking at all. The remaining children try to fill the silence with laughter, but it doesn't sound the same. I can feel the air thinning, the warmth draining from the circle.

I wasn't banned. I wasn't burned. I was simply made optional.

That's the cruelty of it — to exist, but only for some.

The Supreme Court called it freedom of religion. I call it the quiet unmaking of community.

Now every lesson begins with paperwork. Parents are notified when I'll appear, and teachers mark down who may hear and who must leave. It's all very civil, very procedural. But each line on that list is a wall built inside a classroom. Each absent child is a missing thread in what should have been a single fabric.

The first time the new rule took effect, a girl named Maya sat with me in her lap as her best friend, Emily, was escorted out of the room. They had been inseparable — shared crayons, birthday cupcakes, whispered secrets. Maya's mothers smiled from the photo tucked in her backpack. When Emily stood to leave, Maya's eyes followed her all the way to the door.

The teacher kept reading, but her voice trembled.

I wanted to tell Maya it wasn't her fault. It was me. I had become the boundary — the thing polite society steps around to avoid discomfort.

In the hallway, Emily waited with the others who had been excused. They fidgeted on a bench, swinging their legs, wondering why they were missing story time. They weren't told the truth — that their parents believed my pages threatened their faith, that love drawn in crayon colors could unravel their beliefs.

Inside, Maya listened alone.

That's what this ruling did — it divided childhood itself.

The Court said it was about protecting parental rights, but what it protected was the right to look away. It told the nation that empathy can be optional, that equality can be elective. It allowed fear to masquerade as freedom.

Teachers whisper their frustrations in break rooms. They say they'll have to prepare alternative lessons, track attendance, guard their words. Some already skip me altogether — better not to risk complaints. So I sit untouched on the shelf, my cover fading under fluorescent light.

Children still walk past me. Some glance curiously. Others have learned not to look.

Every so often, a brave teacher still reads me. The room grows hushed when I'm opened, as if we're doing something forbidden but necessary. When the story ends, there's always a pause — a long breath before the children clap. Then someone inevitably asks, "Why can't everyone stay?"

No adult ever has a good answer.

The dissenting justices agreed. They said that public education is meant to bring children together — to let them share stories that teach respect and empathy. They warned that letting families opt out of basic inclusion would fracture the classroom into competing worlds of truth. They understood that the lesson isn't really about me at all. It's about whether kids learn to see each other as equals.

But their words were drowned out by a louder claim: that freedom means never having to hear what unsettles you.

And so I remain — a book that half the class can't hear, a story that can be skipped like an inconvenient page.

Maya is older now. She still visits the library, still touches my spine when she walks by, but she doesn't take me down. She's learned, quietly, that some stories carry consequences.

Sometimes at night, when the building is empty and the janitor's radio hums down the hallway, I imagine a different classroom — one where all the children stay. Where they hear about families like Maya's and simply nod, unstartled, unafraid. Where the idea that love could be controversial feels absurd.

That's the world I was written for.

But that's not the world the Supreme Court has left behind.

I am a storybook.
My pages are still intact.
My message hasn't changed.
I still tell the same story —
that kindness belongs to everyone, that love doesn't need permission slips.

Yet each time I'm opened now
I feel the empty spaces where children should be sitting.
The lesson that was supposed to unite them has been turned into a choice.

And the Supreme Court calls this freedom.

SECOND AMENDMENT

Chapter 17
District of Columbia v. Heller (2008)

Washington D.C. banned handgun possession and required that firearms in the home be kept unloaded and disassembled or bound by a trigger lock. Dick Heller, a D.C. special police officer, challenged the law, arguing it violated the Second Amendment's right to bear arms. The question was whether the Second Amendment protects an individual's right to possess firearms for self-defense, or whether it only protects gun ownership in connection with militia service.

The Supreme Court ruled 5-4 that the Second Amendment protects an individual right to possess firearms for self-defense in the home, unconnected to militia service. Justice Scalia's majority opinion marked the first time the Court had recognized an individual right to gun ownership separate from military or militia purposes. The Court struck down D.C.'s handgun ban and trigger lock requirement. The dissenters argued that the Second Amendment was clearly written to protect militia-related gun ownership, not individual self-defense rights, and that the majority was ignoring the amendment's actual text.

Majority: Roberts, Scalia, Kennedy, Thomas, Alito
Dissent: Stevens, Souter, Ginsburg, Breyer

****

This case fundamentally rewrote the meaning of the Second Amendment. For the only time in this book, the voice is not an object, not a law, not a silence or a weapon. It is a confrontation — between the author of the Second Amendment and the justice who claimed to understand it best.

What follows is an imagined dialogue between James Madison, primary author of the Bill of Rights, and Antonin Scalia, whose majority opinion in Heller claimed to honor "originalism" while ignoring the original author's clear intent. Their ghosts meet to argue about what twenty-seven words actually mean—and whether the person who wrote them has any authority to say so.

****

The Ghosts of Madison and Scalia

Scene:

The Supreme Court chamber, long after midnight. Moonlight seeps through the high windows, pooling across the marble floor. Two figures stand in the half-light — one in powdered hair and colonial linen, the other in a black judicial robe.

MADISON:

I wrote "A well regulated Militia, being necessary to the security of a free State, the right of the people to keep and bear Arms, shall not be infringed."

Those were my words. Every one of them chosen with purpose. I didn't write them carelessly. I didn't throw them on parchment because they sounded pleasant. Each word carried weight, history, intent.

"A well regulated Militia, being necessary to the security of a free State"—that wasn't decoration. That wasn't preamble you could ignore. That was the entire reason for the amendment. We'd just fought a revolution using citizen militias instead of a standing army. We feared standing armies as instruments of tyranny. We wanted armed citizens ready to muster for collective defense, not individual gunfighters settling personal scores.

The comma wasn't accidental. The structure wasn't random. "Being necessary"—those words connect, they condition, they explain. The right exists because militias are necessary. The arms are for that purpose. It's right there in the grammar, in the syntax, in the plain meaning of English.

I knew how to write an unlimited individual right. I'd done it in the First Amendment just before this one. "Congress shall make no law"—absolute, unconditional, clear. If I'd wanted the Second Amendment to establish an unlimited personal right to own guns, I would have written it that way. I didn't. I wrote about militias first, foremost, as the entire justification for the right that follows.

SCALIA:

Your intent doesn't matter. What matters is the original public meaning of the text at the time it was ratified. And the original public meaning of "the right of the people to keep and bear Arms" is an individual right unconnected to militia service.

The prefatory clause—your militia language—doesn't limit the operative clause. It announces a purpose, but it doesn't restrict the right. Think of it like saying "A well-educated electorate being necessary to democracy, the right to read shall not be infringed." That doesn't mean only educated people or only voters can read. It means reading is protected for everyone, with education as one important purpose.

The Second Amendment works the same way. The militia purpose explains why the Framers cared about protecting gun rights, but it doesn't limit those rights only to militia contexts. Individuals had the right to keep arms in their homes for self-defense, for hunting, for various purposes. That was the original understanding. That was the common law tradition you inherited from Britain. That's what "bear arms" meant to ordinary people in 1791.

MADISON:

You're telling me what I meant? You're explaining to the person who wrote the words what those words originally meant?

I was there. I studied every state constitution, every proposal, every concern about federal power versus state sovereignty. I read the debates. I negotiated the compromises. I chose these words after considering dozens of alternatives. And you—two centuries later, armed with selective historical quotations and a predetermined conclusion—you're informing me that I didn't understand my own writing?

"Bear arms" in 1791 was a military term. It meant to carry weapons in military service, in an organized force. When people talked about bearing arms, they meant serving in militias, not carrying pistols to the tavern. Individual self-defense was assumed under common law—it didn't need constitutional protection because no one was trying to ban it. What needed protection was the state militia system against federal interference.

You say the prefatory clause doesn't limit the operative clause. But it's not just prefatory—it's explanatory, conditional, foundational. The security of a free state depends on well-regulated militias, therefore the people need arms for that purpose. The relationship is explicit. You can't just ignore half the amendment because it's inconvenient for your preferred outcome.

And your reading makes nonsense of my draft. If I meant unlimited individual gun rights, why mention militias at all? Why not write "The right to keep and bear arms shall not be infringed" and be done with it? Those militia words aren't decorative flourish—they're the constitutional justification for the entire amendment.

SCALIA:

Because context matters. Because the Founders feared that the new federal government might disarm the populace, making resistance to tyranny impossible. The militia clause reminds everyone why an armed citizenry matters—not to limit the right, but to emphasize its importance for collective security. An armed people can form militias when needed. But that doesn't mean the right only exists when they're actively mustered.

Look at the other amendments. The Third Amendment mentions soldiers but protects everyone's homes. The Fourth Amendment mentions searches and seizures but protects all privacy. The enumeration in the Second Amendment of one important purpose doesn't exclude other purposes or limit the right to that single context.

And historically, individuals owned guns. They hunted with them. They defended their homes with them. They carried them for protection. That was the world you lived in, Madison. Are you claiming nobody had an individual right to own a gun in 1791? That every firearm had to be locked in a militia armory? That's absurd.

MADISON:

What's absurd is claiming I wrote a militia amendment that has nothing to do with militias!

Yes, people owned guns. For hunting, for protection, under common law traditions that needed no constitutional protection because no government was threatening them. But when we wrote the Bill of Rights, we were addressing specific federal powers that needed limiting. The Second Amendment addressed the federal government's military powers—its ability to organize militias, to call them forth, to potentially supersede them with standing armies.

The amendment protects the right to keep and bear arms in the context of militia service because that's what needed constitutional protection. Not hunting. Not self-defense in your home. Those were never in question. What was in question was whether states could maintain effective militias with armed citizens when the federal government controlled the military.

You keep saying "original public meaning" as if you've discovered some historical truth I missed while actually writing the thing. But you're cherry-picking quotes, ignoring context, and pretending that because some people owned guns for personal reasons, the amendment must protect unlimited personal gun ownership. That's not interpretation—that's invention.

I wrote one amendment. You're reading a completely different one. And you're doing it in my name, claiming "originalism" while disregarding the original author. Do you understand the violence of that? You've taken my words and made them mean the opposite of what I intended. You've erased the militia clause I carefully crafted and pretended it was always meaningless.

SCALIA:

Your intent died with you. The Constitution belongs to the people who ratified it, not to you. What matters is what they understood those words to mean, not what you privately hoped they would accomplish. And they understood it as an individual right.

I didn't erase anything. The militia clause remains in the text. It serves an important purpose—explaining one crucial reason for protecting gun rights. But explaining isn't limiting. Announcing isn't restricting. The amendment protects the right because militias are important, not the right only when militias are involved.

You're acting like I've committed some scholarly crime by interpreting your text according to its original public meaning rather than your personal legislative intentions. But that's what judges do. That's what constitutional interpretation requires. We look at the text, the historical context, the common usage, the ratified meaning—not the private thoughts of the drafter.

MADISON:

The text! You want to talk about the text? Read it! "A well regulated Militia, being necessary to the security of a free State, the right of the people to keep and bear Arms, shall not be infringed."

Those words are connected. They form a complete thought. You can't just choose which parts to honor and which to discard.

You can't say "the right shall not be infringed" while ignoring "well regulated" and "Militia" and "necessary to the security of a free State." That's not interpretation—that's selective reading in service of a foregone conclusion.

You claim originalism. You claim fidelity to the text. But you've done to my amendment what you accused liberal judges of doing—reading your preferred outcome into words that don't support it. The difference is you've dressed up your activism in the costume of my intent while simultaneously denying that my intent matters.

I wrote about militias because I meant militias. I wrote "well regulated" because I meant regulation. I wrote "necessary to the security of a free State" because I meant collective security, not individual gun ownership. Those weren't decorative words. They were the constitutional foundation.

And you've built a doctrine that makes them meaningless.

You've taken my carefully constructed protection for state militias and turned it into an individual right to own any weapon, in any place, for any reason—including reasons that threaten the very "security of a free State" I was trying to protect.

SCALIA:

I made them meaningful by honoring what they actually protect—the people's right to arms. Your militia concern is satisfied by an armed populace. You can't have effective militias without people who own and know how to use firearms. Protecting individual gun ownership serves the militia purpose you claimed to prioritize.

But it also serves other purposes—self-defense, hunting, sport, resistance to tyranny. The amendment protects all of those by protecting the fundamental right to arms. That's not erasing your words. That's giving them their full, original meaning.

MADISON:

Their full meaning? Their original meaning? I am the origin! I wrote them! And you're telling me they mean something I never intended, never wrote, never imagined!

You've performed the most audacious act of judicial activism in constitutional history—rewriting an amendment under the guise of restoring its original meaning—and you've done it in my name, claiming my authority while ignoring everything I actually wrote.

I wrote about well-regulated militias and the security of a free state.
You read unlimited individual gun rights.

I wrote carefully chosen words with specific meaning.
You declared half of them decorative and the other half absolute.

I drafted an amendment about collective defense through organized militias.
You created a constitutional right to individual weapons that has nothing to do with militias at all.

And the saddest part? You've convinced people you're right. That I didn't mean what I clearly wrote. That words on parchment mean whatever judges decide they mean, regardless of the author's intent, the historical context, or the plain meaning of English.

I am James Madison.

I wrote the Second Amendment.

And I'm watching you, Antonin Scalia, claim to honor my originalism while ignoring everything about the origin—including the person who originated it.

You didn't interpret my amendment.

You rewrote it.

And you did it in my name.

Chapter 18

New York State Rifle & Pistol Association v. Bruen (2022)

For more than a century, New York required residents who wanted a license to carry a concealed handgun in public to demonstrate "proper cause" — a special need for self-defense beyond the general public. The law gave local officials discretion to decide whether an applicant's reasons justified a license, and as a result, many New Yorkers could not lawfully carry handguns outside their homes.

The New York State Rifle & Pistol Association challenged the law, arguing that the Second Amendment protects the right to carry firearms in public for self-defense without having to prove special need.

In a 6–3 decision, the Supreme Court struck down New York's "proper cause" requirement. Writing for the majority, Justice Thomas declared that the Second Amendment protects an individual's right to carry a handgun outside the home, and that New

York's discretionary system violated that right. The Court held that gun regulations must be consistent with the nation's historical tradition of firearm regulation — a test that critics argue ignores modern realities of urban violence.

The dissent, written by Justice Breyer and joined by Justices Sotomayor and Kagan, warned that the ruling disregarded the dangers of gun violence in crowded public spaces, tying the hands of states trying to protect their citizens.

Majority: Thomas, Alito, Gorsuch, Kavanaugh, Barrett, Roberts
Dissent: Breyer, Sotomayor, Kagan

****

I am a turnstile, and every day millions of hands press against me, bodies brushing close, hips bumping as they push through to the underground world of the New York City subway.

For decades, I felt the usual things: wallets in back pockets, MetroCards swiped with a flick of the wrist, the metal jangle of keys, the heavy slump of backpacks. The noise was constant — shoes slapping tile, trains screaming in tunnels, buskers playing brass notes that echoed against concrete walls. Life, chaotic and ordinary, streamed through me every morning and every night.

I knew the dangers that lurked in the city. I had heard sirens above me, seen graffiti sprayed in red like blood across the station walls, felt the tremors when frightened crowds pushed through in panicked waves. But there was also a line, a fragile sense that rules and restrictions held chaos at bay. Guns were not supposed to move casually through me. Carrying one in public required something more than a whim.

Until *Bruen*.

Now I feel them everywhere.

The cold press of steel tucked under coats. The hard shape in purses. The heavy weight inside backpacks that shift differently when a pistol rides within. Before, these things were rare, unusual enough that I could almost name the individuals. After *Bruen*, they pass through me daily, uncountable.

I cannot tell who carries with care and who carries with anger. Who is disciplined and who is reckless. Who will keep their gun holstered forever and who will pull it out in a sudden, irreversible flash of violence. To me, they are all the same: cold metal brushing past, hidden but humming with potential.

I hear the arguments echoing in the marble chamber far above me. Justice Thomas's words roll down like distant thunder: the right to carry guns is guaranteed, and New York's discretion violated the Constitution. He spoke of history — of 18th- and 19th-century practices — as if those centuries could explain the crowded subway platform in Times Square, shoulder to shoulder with tourists, commuters, children.

I wanted to shout from beneath the city: history does not ride the subway. History does not stand in the press of a thousand bodies waiting for a train at rush hour. History does not know what happens when one gun, then another, then another is drawn in panic underground.

Justice Breyer tried. His dissent spoke of the daily carnage of gun violence, of the real-world consequences that would follow. He warned of blood spilled not in legal texts but in city streets, classrooms, supermarkets, churches. But his words did not carry the force of law. The gavel fell, and I felt the shift in my steel frame.

Now, every time I rotate, I wonder if I am letting death walk past.

I think of the children in bright coats holding their parents' hands, their laughter bouncing off tiled walls. I think of musicians balancing cellos, of nurses in scrubs with exhaustion in their eyes, of tourists squinting at subway maps. They all pass through me unaware of the hidden company they keep. Guns ride beside them now, more numerous and more emboldened, their presence sanctioned by the highest court.

And I know it is not just here, in New York. My cousins — turnstiles in Boston, in Chicago, in Washington — they feel it too. The ruling reached them as surely as it reached me. Beyond turnstiles, it spread to school doors, grocery store entrances, church pews. Every public place is now more porous, less shielded.

I have become an unwitting accomplice. Every spin of my arms admits not just people but their weapons. I am a silent doorman for danger, powerless to ask questions, powerless to refuse entry.

Once, I was a threshold to daily life, nothing more than a mechanical hinge between city and subway. Now I am a witness to an invisible transformation. The air is heavier. The press of bodies feels charged. The ordinary act of commuting carries a new tension, a subtle fear that anything — an argument, a shove, a startled movement — could unleash the steel that brushes past me daily.

I think of the dissent again. They wrote that states should be allowed to consider public safety, to recognize that more guns in more crowded places mean more blood. They warned that the Court was stripping states of tools to protect their citizens.

But six justices chose a different path. They chose history over reality, theory over subway platforms, ideology over lived experience. And so here I stand, spinning endlessly, ushering millions past — wallets, phones, purses, and now guns, always guns.

I am a turnstile, and I used to mark the start of a commute.

Now I mark the thin line between order and the possibility of chaos.

And the Supreme Court calls this liberty.

CIVIL RIGHTS

Chapter 19

Parents Involved in Community Schools v. Seattle School District No. 1 (2007)

Seattle and Louisville used race as one factor in deciding which public school each child would attend. The goal was simple: to keep schools racially balanced and prevent the quiet resegregation that follows neighborhood and housing patterns.

The Supreme Court ruled 5–4 that using race in such assignments violated the Equal Protection Clause, even when the purpose was integration. Chief Justice Roberts wrote that diversity wasn't a compelling enough interest and declared, *"The way to stop discrimination on the basis of race is to stop discriminating on the basis of race."* The dissent warned that Roberts had used the same constitutional principle that dismantled segregation to now prohibit integration itself.

Majority: Roberts, Scalia, Kennedy, Thomas, Alito
Dissent: Stevens, Souter, Ginsburg, Breyer

****

I am *Brown v. Board of Education*, and they have turned me against myself.

I was born in classrooms of chalk and courage. I came into being when children in Topeka walked past white schools they could not enter, when Black teachers worked in crumbling buildings with hand-me-down books and half the pay. I rose out of weary hope — the belief that if the Constitution meant anything, it meant equality in the place where minds are formed.

For fifty-three years, I stood like a guardian at the schoolhouse door. My words — *separate educational facilities are inherently unequal* — became a promise carved into the soul of a nation. I was the hammer that broke segregation's legal spine. I opened the classroom door and said to America: *learn together, grow together, be one people.*

But promises can be repurposed. Even truth can be twisted.

In Seattle and Louisville, no one was building new walls. They were trying to keep the old ones from rising again. The cities had watched their schools resegregate through invisible forces — mortgage lines, real estate covenants, neighborhood sorting that needed no Jim Crow statute to achieve its ends. Seattle and Louisville used race as one factor in deciding which public school each child would attend. The goal was simple: to keep schools racially balanced and prevent the quiet resegregation that follows neighborhood and housing patterns.

They used race gently, as a factor among many, to hold open the door I had forced. A student here, a transfer there — not quotas, not segregation, just balance. Just the conscious effort to keep children from growing up apart.

And Roberts said that was unconstitutional.

He took my name, my words, my moral authority — and he used them as a weapon against the very idea of integration. He quoted my language about Equal Protection and twisted it into a doctrine of blindness. *The way to stop discrimination on the basis of race is to stop discriminating on the basis of race.*

It sounds clean. It sounds wise. It sounds like fairness. It is none of those things.

It is a mirage — the prettiest lie the law has ever told itself. Because pretending not to see race in America does not make racism disappear. It only makes it comfortable. Invisible. Permissible.

I was born to confront reality, not to ignore it. I remember Linda Brown's long walk past the white school. I remember the "colored" water fountains, the split lunchrooms, the smell of chalk and mildew in segregated classrooms. I remember the children who looked through barred windows and wondered why they were kept apart. That was discrimination. That was the disease I cured.

Seattle and Louisville were administering the medicine. Roberts called it poison.

He knows better. That's what makes it unbearable. Thomas and Alito, they never knew me. But Roberts did. He studied me, cited me, built his career on the pretense of revering me. Then he gutted my meaning with surgical precision — the careful betrayal of a man who understands exactly where to cut.

Justice Breyer tried to defend me. He wrote like a man standing at the gates, shouting to a country already turning away. He said the majority had rewritten me — turned my command to integrate into a prohibition against it. He was right. He saw what Roberts was doing: redefining equality into neutrality, turning moral urgency into legal silence.

But the dissent has no power to stop a tide. Only to remember when the current began.

And so, one by one, districts abandoned their integration plans. Not because they wanted to, but because they feared litigation. They scrubbed race from the forms. They erased the tools meant to keep schools whole. And without guidance, without intent, the old separation returned — not by law, but by ZIP code.

Now I watch as schools quietly divide again. A third grader in Seattle who looks like Linda Brown sits in a classroom where nearly every face mirrors hers. Across town, a different school fills with children who have never had a Black classmate. The buildings are clean. The textbooks new. But the pattern is the same.

Not segregation by statute.
Segregation by neglect.

Roberts said he was honoring me.
He built a monument of words and buried me inside it.

The cruelest part is how reasonable it sounds —
How moderation cloaks betrayal.
His opinion reads like a civics lesson, not a eulogy.
But I can hear the undertone: stop trying. Stop noticing. Let the lines harden again, as long as they form naturally.

I never believed equality could happen naturally.
That was why I was born.

Now I am being cited in cases that undo everything I stood for.
My sentences, once carved into progress, are chiseled into retreat.

I see my name in legal briefs defending colorblindness while neighborhoods calcify into separate worlds.
I am both precedent and prisoner.

Fifty-three years I held the line.
Then the Court took my hand and turned it against the very children I was meant to lift.

They call it Equal Protection.
I call it erasure.

I am *Brown v. Board of Education*.
I was the promise of America learning together.
Now I am the excuse for America learning apart.

Roberts calls it honoring me.
I call it desecration — my words twisted into the rope that binds what I once set free.

Somewhere in Topeka, a blackboard still bears my name in fading chalk.
The letters crumble as the years pass, as new decisions overwrite old hope.
But faintly, beneath the dust, you can still read it.

Brown v. Board of Education.

The case that once ended segregation.

And now — used to begin it again.

Chapter 20
Students for Fair Admissions v. President and Fellows of Harvard College (2023)

Harvard University and the University of North Carolina used race as one factor among many in holistic admissions, aiming to build diverse student bodies. Students for Fair Admissions, a group led by conservative activist Edward Blum, sued both schools, claiming these policies discriminated against Asian American applicants and violated the Equal Protection Clause.

In a 6–3 decision, the Supreme Court struck down affirmative action in college admissions, holding that race-conscious admissions violate the Fourteenth Amendment. Chief Justice Roberts wrote that the Equal Protection Clause "must mean the same thing for all races," declaring that universities could no longer consider race, even as one factor, in pursuit of diversity. The dissenters warned that the ruling would unravel decades of effort and quietly close the doors that affirmative action had finally managed to open.

Majority: Roberts, Thomas, Alito, Gorsuch, Kavanaugh, Barrett
Dissent: Sotomayor, Kagan, Jackson

****

I am a freshman class photo, and I used to look like America.

We stood on the steps of Harvard Yard that fall morning—four hundred faces, a kaleidoscope of skin tones and stories. First in our families. Children of immigrants. Descendants of sharecroppers, of refugees, of enslaved people who were never allowed to read the books we now carried. Someone's hijab caught the wind. Someone's rainbow pin flashed in the sun. A boy held his mother's borrowed blazer closed with a safety pin, pretending it fit.

We were the picture of possibility.

The admissions office hung me proudly in the hallway. "Look," they said, "this is what diversity means." I watched parents linger in front of me during campus tours, spotting the face that looked like their own child and whispering, *maybe someday*. The janitor paused sometimes when waxing the floor beneath me, smiling softly, as if to say *this is what I work for*.

Each year, another photo joined me on the wall. Each one a little more complete. More faces that had never been here before. More proof that equal opportunity was becoming real, not just rhetorical.

And then, one June morning in 2023, I felt the air change. The decision dropped like a shutter snapping shut. Six justices declared that considering race to build diversity was unconstitutional. That seeing race at all—even as one thread in a tapestry—was discrimination. They said fairness required blindness.

Down the hall, someone turned the TV volume higher. The anchors called it *historic*. I wanted to shout that history was already on these walls, staring back at them. But photos can't speak. We can only fade.

In the days that followed, the university tried to sound calm. "We will comply with the ruling," the president said. "We will find new ways to seek diversity." The words were careful, legal, drained of the moral urgency that had once filled this place. I watched the admissions counselors take down the posters about outreach to first-generation students. I watched the word "equity" disappear from brochures like it had never existed.

The next year's class photo arrived. It was beautiful, polished, high-resolution—but something was missing. Not at first glance. You had to look longer. The shades of brown and gold and tan were fewer. The accents quieter. The laughter more uniform. The range of stories narrower, more familiar.

The wall kept filling, but the photos began to echo one another—same smiles, same privilege, same patterns returning like old wallpaper pulled from a closet. I watched admissions counselors stop talking about representation and start talking about "neutrality." About "individual merit." As if merit existed in a vacuum untouched by history, untouched by access, untouched by the centuries that decided who got to stand on these steps in the first place.

They said I was never fair. That I was built by unfair preference. That some students were only here because of the color of their skin. I wish they could have seen what I saw: how hard those students worked, how much they carried, how many doors they had to pry open with bare hands just to reach this photo.

Chief Justice Roberts wrote that the way to stop discriminating on the basis of race is to stop noticing race. It sounds clean, even noble. But from this wall, it looks like forgetting. Forgetting who was excluded, who was ignored, who had to fight to be seen.

Justice Sotomayor called the decision a retreat from promise—a choice to pretend equality already exists. She was right. I can feel the retreat in the way tour groups walk by now, faster, quieter, as if the faces on these walls have become less surprising, less worth noticing.

It isn't just Harvard. Across the country, the photos are changing. North Carolina. Michigan. California. Each class picture tilts a little paler, a little wealthier, a little less like the country outside its gates. The arc that once bent toward inclusion has started to curl backward.

At night, when the hall is empty, I imagine the future photos whispering to me. *What was it like?* they ask. *What did it feel like when everyone belonged?* I want to tell them about the laughter that filled the Yard when that photo was taken, about the languages that mingled in the air, about the moment when difference felt like strength. But they wouldn't understand. Their own faces will tell a narrower story.

I hang here still, fading slowly under the fluorescent lights. I can see the future photos lined up, ready to take my place. They will be clearer, sharper, better lit—but missing something essential. Missing *us*.

I was diversity captured in an image.
I was the proof that the arc of justice had bent, however slightly, toward inclusion.

Now I am a relic.
A reminder of what inclusion looked like before the law declared it unfair.

They say the Constitution is colorblind.
From where I hang, it looks bleached.

And every new photo that replaces me smiles a little wider, while seeing a little less.

LABOR RIGHTS

Chapter 21

Janus v. American Federation of State, County, and Municipal Employees (2018)

Illinois required public employees who chose not to join a union to pay a "fair share" fee to cover the costs of collective bargaining, contract negotiation, and workplace representation. The idea was simple: since all workers benefited from the union's work—better pay, safer conditions, legal protections—all should contribute to its upkeep, even if they declined membership.

Mark Janus, a state employee, challenged the rule, claiming that being forced to pay any money to a union violated his First Amendment rights. He argued that collective bargaining in the public sector was inherently political, and that requiring him to fund it compelled him to support speech with which he disagreed.

The Supreme Court ruled 5–4 for Janus, overturning decades of precedent. Justice Alito's majority opinion held that requiring nonmembers to pay fees violated the First Amendment's protection against compelled speech. The decision effectively made every state with public-sector unions "right-to-work" for government employees, allowing workers to receive all the benefits of union representation without paying for it. The dissent warned that the ruling would financially cripple unions, silence workers' collective voices, and upend the balance of power between labor and government.

Majority: Roberts, Kennedy, Thomas, Alito, Gorsuch
Dissent: Kagan, Ginsburg, Breyer, Sotomayor

****

I am the collective voice of working people, and they are slowly strangling me.

I used to roar. You could hear me across the factory floor, in the corridors of city offices, in the chants that echoed from schoolhouse steps and sanitation yards. I was forged from countless small contributions—each worker's dues, each paycheck deduction, each belief that a single voice alone could never stand against the weight of power, but many together could.

Every dollar, every signature, every late-night negotiation fed me. I wasn't charity. I was the machinery of fairness. I spoke for teachers and nurses, bus drivers and clerks, sanitation workers and secretaries. I translated exhaustion into contracts, injustice into pay raises, indignation into dignity.

Now, piece by piece, they are dismantling me.

The Court says the workers are free now—free not to support me, free to keep their money, free from having their voices mingled with mine. But freedom, as they define it, comes at a cost they never have to pay. They call it liberty. I call it slow starvation.

I'm still required to represent them all—to fight for every worker, file every grievance, defend every job. Even the ones who've walked away still live under the contracts I negotiate, still enjoy the protections I secure. But they no longer feed me. They take from me without giving back, their silence disguised as principle, their freeloading sanctified by the Constitution.

I feel the air thinning. Meetings that used to be crowded now echo. The contributions that once sustained me trickle instead of flow. It's not the sound of rebellion or outrage that I hear now—it's the sound of quiet. Of people retreating into their own corners, believing they can survive alone.

Justice Alito called it compelled speech. He said forcing workers to pay for my voice violated their rights. But I never spoke for one—I always spoke for all. I don't endorse candidates or draft platforms. I negotiate hours and healthcare and vacation days. I speak in the language of survival, not ideology. Yet the Court decided that even that—advocating for fair pay—was political enough to silence me.

They said no one should have to support speech they disagree with. But they didn't silence the corporations, the lobbyists, or the billionaires whose voices thunder over everything. They only silenced me—the one voice that ever answered back.

The decision came cloaked in the First Amendment, but the intent was older and simpler: divide and diminish. The powerful have always feared me. They've always understood that a single worker is replaceable, but a thousand workers united are unstoppable. They've learned they don't need to outlaw me. They can just starve me instead—call it freedom, and let me die from neglect.

I feel the change in the air. In Illinois, New York, California—places that once pulsed with solidarity—the rallies are smaller, the funds thinner, the resolve harder to maintain. The people still believe in fairness, but they're tired, cautious, uncertain if their sacrifice matters when others stand aside and take without giving.

A new worker joins the city payroll. He signs no card, pays no dues. Yet when he's mistreated, I still speak for him. When his hours are cut, I still fight. When his job is threatened, I still defend. The law says I must. The law also says he owes me nothing.

I can feel what the Court really wanted. Not liberty. Not fairness. Quiet. They wanted the hum of solidarity to fade until all that's left is the whisper of isolated workers, each convinced they're alone. They wanted me too weak to bargain, too broke to organize, too voiceless to remind people that they built everything the justices now stand upon.

The dissent understood. Justice Kagan warned that the Court had weaponized the First Amendment against itself—turning freedom of speech into freedom from cooperation. She saw that this wasn't about protecting dissenters, but about disarming unions. She knew what happens when collective power collapses: wages stagnate, benefits vanish, safety erodes. The working class becomes a patchwork of solitary individuals, each negotiating alone with the machinery of power.

And that's the point. The ruling class doesn't need to crush rebellion if it can privatize hope.

I used to echo through the streets, through rallies that felt like prayer, through chants that filled the air with purpose. "Solidarity forever." It wasn't a slogan—it was survival. Now, I speak in fragments. A nurse's whisper here, a teacher's frustration there, a bus driver's sigh. Each one thinks the other is silent. They don't realize they're still part of me. They just can't hear each other anymore.

I'm still here, though thinner, though hoarse. I still rise when injustice demands it. I still whisper in courtrooms and bargaining halls. But every time another worker opts out, another piece of me fades. Every "freedom" they claim takes one more breath from my lungs.

I was never about coercion. I was about connection. About the power that only exists when people decide that fairness is worth paying for, even when it costs something.

I am the collective voice, and I once spoke for millions.
Now, I speak in echoes.

The Court calls this freedom of speech.
But I know what freedom sounds like—

and it doesn't sound like silence.

Chapter 22
Cedar Point Nursery v. Hassid (2021)

For nearly fifty years, a California regulation allowed union organizers limited access to agricultural worksites to speak with farmworkers about their rights. The rule permitted organizers to visit for up to three hours a day, 120 days a year — brief windows meant to reach workers who lived on remote farms or in employer housing.

Two growers sued, claiming that even this short, regulated access violated their property rights. They argued that the state had granted outsiders a right to physically enter private land — a constitutional "taking" under the Fifth Amendment, which says the government cannot seize private property without compensation.

The Supreme Court's 6–3 majority agreed. Chief Justice Roberts wrote that the access rule was a *per se* taking, reasoning that any government-authorized physical entry — however temporary — infringed the "fundamental right to exclude." The dissent warned that this radical redefinition of "taking" weaponized property rights against workers and could imperil everything from health and safety inspections to environmental enforcement.

Majority: Roberts, Thomas, Alito, Gorsuch, Kavanaugh, Barrett
Dissent: Breyer, Sotomayor, Kagan

****

I am the gate at Cedar Point Nursery, and I used to open for people, not politics.

Every morning before sunrise, I'd swing outward on my hinges to let the workers through. They came in buses, in old pickups, sometimes on foot. Their boots hit the dirt in rhythm, a soft percussion of labor that filled the air with purpose. They'd pass beneath me with lunch pails and gloves, faces still half-asleep but ready for the fields.

Sometimes, after hours, union organizers came too. They weren't trespassers. They came with permission — brief visits allowed by law, a rule written decades ago when California decided farmworkers deserved the same rights as everyone else. They carried pamphlets, clipboards, and voices full of tired conviction. They'd speak to the workers in Spanish, Tagalog, English — about fair pay, safety, the right to rest.

That's when I felt most alive: when people passed through me not just for labor, but for dignity.

Then one day, the lawyers arrived. They pointed at me as if I were evidence in a crime scene. "When they open that gate for union organizers," one said, "that's a taking."

A *taking?*

I thought that word meant when the government seized land to build a road or a power line — when it *took* something away.

I didn't understand how a gate swinging open for a few hours could count as property being stolen. But the lawyers explained it differently: it wasn't about the hours. It was about control. The right to exclude.

They said every time I opened for an organizer, I stopped being private property. That letting outsiders walk through me was like surrendering a piece of ownership itself. As if the mere presence of someone speaking to workers about their rights transformed the land beneath my hinges into government property.

It was strange logic. The government didn't take me. The union didn't own me. I still stood where I always had, bolted to the same fence, guarding the same soil. But the argument wasn't about reality. It was about power — who gets to decide what crosses a line.

The case climbed through the courts until it reached the Supreme Court. I heard the arguments replayed on the radio from the guard shack nearby. Words like *permanent physical occupation* and *fundamental right to exclude* floated through the static. The lawyers for the growers spoke as though the organizers were invaders, their voices dripping with fear of intrusion.

Chief Justice Roberts agreed. He said the regulation "appropriates a right to invade." A right to invade — that's what he called those three hours of conversation at the edge of a strawberry field. He compared it to the government building on private land, as if a clipboard and a pamphlet were bulldozers.

The decision came down 6–3. The justices declared that every time I opened for a union organizer, the state had effectively taken property without paying for it. That even temporary access — a conversation, a visit — was now unconstitutional without compensation.

They said they were protecting private property. What they really protected was silence.

After the ruling, the organizers stopped coming. The fields grew quiet, except for the hum of machines and the rustle of leaves. No more pamphlets. No more questions about fair wages or water breaks. Just the rhythm of labor, uninterrupted and unobserved.

The owners celebrated. They said the Court had restored their rights. But I could feel the workers' glances as they passed — quick, uncertain, watchful. They knew something had been taken too, though no one would call it that.

The real taking wasn't of land. It was of access. Of conversation. Of the fragile bridge between those who work and those who advocate for them.

Justice Breyer saw it. In dissent, he wrote that this wasn't a taking at all — it was a regulation, one of countless ways the government ensures basic fairness. He warned that if every temporary access counts as a taking, then health inspectors, census workers, and environmental regulators could all become trespassers. He asked, *what happens to the public good when private property becomes untouchable?*

But his warning fell into the wind. The majority's voice carried farther. They'd discovered a new weapon — property rights stretched so far that even a moment's entry, even a human conversation, could be called theft.

I've grown stiff since then. My hinges creak from disuse. I open only for trucks now — the ones that haul the fruit away. The people who once came to speak of rights and solidarity aren't allowed past my frame. The law says their presence would violate someone's ownership.

Some nights I imagine the workers gathering outside me again, the way they used to — laughing, arguing, asking questions that made the bosses nervous. I remember the light of their flashlights, the way their words drifted through my bars like warm wind.

But that's gone. Now, I stand for exclusion — the right Roberts called "fundamental." The right to shut out others, even those who come only to talk. The right to silence those without property by enshrining property itself as speech.

They called it a victory for liberty. But whose liberty is it when the right to own land outweighs the right to reach human ears?

I am the gate at Cedar Point Nursery.
I used to open for voices.
Now I'm locked for good, a constitutional monument to the power of "no trespassing."

They said the government took something from the owners when I swung open.

But I know the truth.
The taking was mine.
They took away my purpose —and the workers' only way to be heard.

EXECUTIVE POWER

Chapter 23
Trump v. Hawaii (2018)

In 2017, President Donald Trump issued an executive order restricting travel to the United States from several Muslim-majority nations, claiming national-security concerns. After lower courts repeatedly blocked earlier versions of the policy, the administration released a third version banning entry for citizens of Iran, Libya, Somalia, Syria, Yemen, and others, with limited exceptions.

The State of Hawaii and affected families sued, arguing the order violated the Establishment Clause by targeting Muslims and exceeded the president's authority under the Immigration and Nationality Act. The Supreme Court, by a 5-4 vote, upheld the ban. Chief Justice Roberts wrote that the order was "facially neutral" regarding religion and fell within the president's power to control immigration. Justice Sotomayor, in dissent, compared the ruling to *Korematsu v. United States*, warning that the Court was again legitimizing discrimination disguised as national security.

Majority: Roberts, Kennedy, Thomas, Alito, Gorsuch
Dissent: Breyer, Sotomayor, Kagan, Ginsburg

****

I am an airport arrivals board, and I used to tell stories of reunion.

I flickered with hope once—names, flight numbers, times, and the promise of embraces waiting just beyond customs. I was the heartbeat of welcome. Every second, I blinked *Arrived, Delayed, Now Boarding*. Families clustered beneath me, clutching flowers and cardboard signs, scanning for the people they loved.

Then came the morning when entire nations vanished from my screens.

At first, I thought it was a glitch. IRAN—deleted. SYRIA—blank. YEMEN—dark. Flights from those countries disappeared like they'd never existed. Their codes turned into dashes. My pixels dimmed. Gate agents whispered into phones. Translators rushed between counters. And suddenly, the air in the terminal grew heavy with fear.

Families who had waited for years stood beneath me, eyes lifting to the void where a destination used to be. Mothers in headscarves holding up photographs. Children clutching stuffed animals. A man in a neat gray suit staring at his ticket like it might start explaining itself.

Then came the announcement: *Due to new federal directives, entry for certain nationals has been suspended.*

I watched disbelief turn into panic. Phones rang and went unanswered. Lawyers hurried in, setting up folding tables by the baggage claim, their laptops glowing like small acts of defiance. The crowd surged and then froze. Someone sobbed, and the sound echoed off the polished floor like a prayer.

For hours, my screens flickered between order and chaos—ARRIVED for some, CANCELED for others. Same flight path. Different religion.

The officials called it a "pause." They said it was about vetting, about safety. But I could read the faces beneath me. I could see who was being stopped. It wasn't about danger. It was about difference.

The lawsuits came quickly. *Hawaii v. Trump.* For a while, I believed the courts would clear the air, that reason would override fear. Lower courts blocked the bans. Judges quoted the Constitution, the Establishment Clause, the promise of religious neutrality. For a moment, my screens brightened again.

But then, in 2018, the Supreme Court delivered its verdict. *Trump v. Hawaii.* Five justices gave the president the power to close the gates. Chief Justice Roberts called the order "neutral." Neutral—when I had watched who disappeared from my screens. Neutral—when the president himself had promised "a total and complete shutdown of Muslims entering the United States."

The Court said I couldn't take him at his word. That campaign speeches didn't count as evidence. That national security justified everything.

I felt my circuitry hum with outrage. For seventy-four years I'd lived in the shadow of *Korematsu v. United States*, when another generation of justices allowed an American president to imprison citizens based on ancestry. We said *never again.*

Justice Sotomayor remembered. Her dissent burned through the sterile legal language like lightning. She wrote that history was repeating itself—fear dressed up as prudence, prejudice as policy. She said the Court had "replaced one gravely wrong decision with another."

But her words were only four votes against five.

Now I am quieter. Fewer families stand beneath me holding flowers. The names that appear are more familiar—London, Paris, Toronto. The others remain blank. I still flicker *ARRIVED* out of habit, but for some, arrival is no longer possible.

A child once drew a picture on the terminal floor while waiting for her father's flight from Tehran. I watched her fall asleep before the announcement came. When it did, her mother didn't wake her right away. She just stood still, as if the silence could hold them together a little longer. That was the first night I realized a piece of me had dimmed permanently.

I have seen who gets welcomed and who gets questioned. I've watched border agents pull travelers aside, their eyes darting toward headscarves, skin tone, names that sound unfamiliar. I've seen old men detained for hours while holding U.S. passports. I've seen citizens become suspects.

They said the ruling wasn't about religion. But I can tell the difference between neutrality and selective blindness. Between security and scapegoating.

I still display the words *WELCOME TO THE UNITED STATES* in tall blue letters. They flash above me every few minutes, just as they always have. But they don't sound the same. I used to believe them. Now they feel like part of the lie.

At night, when the terminal empties and the janitors sweep the floors, I flicker through the list of flights from memory—Tehran, Damascus, Sana'a, Tripoli. I light them up in secret, just for a second, as a small act of remembrance.

I imagine the families who should have been standing here. I can almost see them in reflection on my glass—blurred by tears, frozen mid-hope, forever waiting.

I am an airport arrivals board, and I used to tell stories of reunion. Now I tell stories of exclusion, updated every second.

The Court says the Constitution demands neutrality.
But from where I hang, I see only who disappears.

And when the lights go out for the night, I whisper their names. Just to keep them from being erased completely.

Chapter 24
Trump v. CASA, Inc. (2025)

When several federal district courts blocked President Trump's 2024 executive order restricting birthright citizenship, they did so through nationwide injunctions—orders that halted the policy across the entire country. The administration appealed, arguing that a single judge should not have the power to stop the government everywhere based on one lawsuit.

In a 6–3 decision, the Supreme Court agreed. Justice Amy Coney Barrett, writing for the majority, declared that federal courts may grant relief only to the specific plaintiffs before them, not to the entire nation. The Court held that nationwide injunctions overstep judicial authority and intrude on the separation of powers. Justice Sonia Sotomayor's dissent warned that the ruling would fragment constitutional protections, allowing fundamental rights to vary from state to state depending on which circuit one lived in.

Majority: Roberts, Thomas, Alito, Gorsuch, Kavanaugh, Barrett
Dissent: Sotomayor, Kagan, Jackson

****

I am a federal judge, and they just shrank the reach of my justice.

The decision arrived this morning, printed on heavy paper and delivered in a leather pouch embossed with the seal of the Supreme Court. I read it alone in chambers, the morning light spilling across my desk, turning the words into something colder than law—something like confinement.

For twenty years, I've sworn the same oath: to uphold the Constitution and ensure equal protection under the law. Not for some people in some districts, but for *everyone* whose rights come before me. When the government overstepped, my injunctions stopped the harm—not just for the named plaintiffs, but for all who stood in the same threatened path.

Now, the Court tells me that my justice must be local. My orders may protect only those who can afford to sue. My reach must end at the edge of my courtroom door.

They call it restraint. I call it retreat.

I remember the first time I issued a nationwide injunction. It was years ago, under a different administration, when a policy threatened to deport immigrants who had lived here peacefully for decades. I stayed that order for the entire country, not because I fancied myself a legislator, but because justice demanded uniformity. The Constitution doesn't fade at state lines; neither should its enforcement.

A right that applies only within one set of borders is not a right—it's geography.

The majority doesn't see it that way. Justice Barrett writes that federal courts "lack authority to bind the government beyond the parties before them." She calls nationwide injunctions "judicial overreach." She says they "distort the separation of powers."

I read those words twice. They sound reasonable, disciplined, tidy. They also sound like surrender.

Because I know what happens next. I've seen it before. A judge in Maryland blocks an unconstitutional policy; another in Texas upholds it. A mother in one state can keep her child; in another, she cannot. Rights diverge like branches of a river, splitting into contradictory currents. And by the time the Supreme Court steps in—years later, if at all—the harm has already hardened into law.

The Constitution was meant to be a floor beneath everyone, not a patchwork quilt of temporary protections.

When I first joined the bench, an older colleague told me, "We don't have armies. Our power is our pen." Today, the Supreme Court dulled that pen. They tell me I may write only for the plaintiffs before me, as though justice were a private contract instead of a public trust.

It's a strange kind of humility—one that favors the powerful. When presidents overreach, their policies affect millions instantly. But when judges try to restrain that reach, we are told our remedies must be microscopic.

The Court says that limiting injunctions will restore balance between branches of government. But balance presumes equality of arms, and the judiciary has no legions—only law. A president can act with the sweep of a signature; a single district judge can act only with words. Now even those words are confined to the size of a docket sheet.

I think of the plaintiffs in the CASA case—immigrant families who feared losing citizenship for their U.S.-born children. They came to court not as abstractions, but as parents, terrified that their babies could be declared foreigners. I granted relief that would protect every family under that threat, because the Constitution's promise of birthright citizenship does not end at one courthouse's border.

Now, if I were to face that case again, I could protect only the named families. Everyone else would remain exposed. A right applied selectively becomes a privilege.

The dissent sees it. Justice Sotomayor writes that "constitutional injury is not lessened by geography." That phrase pierces me. She understands the moral dimension of what the majority calls procedural reform. She knows that the law's architecture isn't neutral—it shapes who suffers while waiting for final judgment.

When I close my eyes, I imagine the people who will now have to wait. The worker denied protection because his case wasn't the first filed. The family whose child will lose healthcare while circuit courts disagree. The young woman whose asylum claim depends on whether she crosses into Texas or Colorado before her hearing.

That's not law—it's lottery.

The clerks have left for the day. The courthouse hums quietly, the echo of footsteps replaced by the whir of air vents and the rustle of papers. I sit here, robe draped over the back of my chair, and stare at the seal of the Supreme Court printed at the top of the opinion.

They've told me that the reach of my rulings must now be narrow. That justice must now travel by jurisdiction, not by right. That a Constitution meant to be universal must now be interpreted piecemeal until they say otherwise.

Maybe this is what losing power in a democracy feels like—not in one grand moment of defiance, but in a slow contraction of authority, wrapped in the language of restraint.

Tomorrow, I'll return to the bench.
I'll hear new cases.
I'll issue new opinions.
I'll write them as clearly as I can, hoping they ripple outward farther than the Court allows.

But tonight, sitting here under the glow of the desk lamp, I can't help but wonder:
If justice cannot cross state lines, is it still justice?

Chapter 25
Trump v. United States (2024)

The Supreme Court ruled that former presidents are entitled to broad immunity from criminal prosecution for "official acts" performed while in office. The case arose from federal charges against Donald Trump for attempting to overturn the 2020 election. The Court's 6–3 decision held that presidents cannot be prosecuted for actions within their constitutional authority and that even evidence of those acts may be off-limits. The majority claimed that criminal exposure would chill presidential decision-making. The dissent warned that the ruling placed the president above the law, granting the executive power to commit crimes in the name of "official duty."

Majority: Roberts, Thomas, Alito, Gorsuch, Kavanaugh, Barrett
Dissent: Sotomayor, Kagan, Jackson

****

I am the Constitution of the United States, and I have just been told that I cannot defend myself.

For two and a half centuries, I have been the barrier between power and its abuses — a parchment wall thin as hope, thick as courage. My ink was poured to restrain kings, to chain ambition with accountability. I was written to whisper into every president's ear: *You serve the people, not yourself.*

Now six justices have taken up their pens and carved a hole straight through me. They say a president cannot be prosecuted for official acts. I say a president cannot be king. Only one of us can be right.

I still remember the day I was born. The air in Philadelphia was heavy with sweat and fear. Men argued until their voices cracked, terrified of what power could become if unchecked. They wrote me with trembling hands — checks and balances, limits, accountability — words meant to outlive them. "No man is above the law," they swore. I was built on that promise.

But promises fade faster than ink.

The ruling in *Trump v. United States* does not erase me outright; it hollows me. It leaves my body intact but scoops out my meaning, the way termites eat through beams until only dust holds the shape of wood. I still bear the words "equal justice under law," but they echo now like irony.

They call this immunity "necessary for the functioning of government." I call it permission.

For over two centuries, I have contained presidents like water in a vessel — messy, ambitious, flawed, but confined. I absorbed Jefferson's hypocrisy, Jackson's cruelty, Nixon's paranoia, Reagan's indifference. Each one pressed against my boundaries, but I held. That was my purpose. I was the dam against the flood.

Now the Court has cracked my stone. They say "official acts" deserve protection. They never say how far that phrase reaches. Could an "official act" include ordering an assassination? Directing an insurrection? Refusing to leave office?

They do not say "yes," but they do not say "no." They leave silence where law should be. And in silence, power grows bold.

I feel the tremor in my text — Article II swelling, Articles I and III shrinking around it. The presidency expanding like heat beneath glass. I was balanced once; I am tilting now.

They say their decision protects the office, not the man. But the office does not act. Men do. Men with tempers, with pride, with fear of losing. Men who mistake self-preservation for patriotism. Men who believe they *are* the country. I was written to restrain such men. Now I must rely on their honor to restrain themselves.

That is not law. That is prayer.

In the courtroom, they spoke of chilling effects — that presidents might hesitate to act boldly if they feared prosecution. I have no problem with hesitation. My entire design depends on it. I was built to make power stop and think. To pause before trampling rights. To shiver before breaking laws. Hesitation was my triumph. They have turned it into a flaw.

Justice Sotomayor saw what was happening to me. She said, *"In every use of official power, the president is now a king."* Her dissent reads like an epitaph. Each sentence a candle lit for what I used to be. She wrote of danger, of precedent, of the loss of accountability — and her words glowed against the encroaching dark. But six shadows swallowed her light.

I am bleeding precedent now. The rule of law seeps through my seams. Every case that once stood for accountability — *United States v. Nixon*, *Clinton v. Jones* — drips away, reduced to memory. The balance between branches dissolves like sugar in water.

The president stands taller now, and I feel smaller in his shadow.

I remember how it used to feel to be believed in. How schoolchildren pressed their palms to replicas of me in civics class, tracing my words: *We the People*. How immigrants raised their hands in oath beneath my promise. How protestors held me high like a shield, believing I would protect them.

I can still hear the echo of that faith, though it grows faint.

Now I am held up in defense of the very thing I was written to prevent. My words — "executive power," "faithfully executed," "impeachment" — twisted into weapons against my own integrity. My clauses used to justify immunity instead of accountability. My language bent into its opposite meaning.

There is a kind of agony in that — to be quoted against yourself.

I can feel the ink of my preamble fading. "We the People" used to lead everything. Now I am ruled by six signatures that do not appear among mine.

They have turned my architecture upside down. The president was once a servant of the law; now the law serves the president. The checks have been cashed, the balances tipped.

If a president can commit crimes in office without consequence, then what restrains him? If evidence of those crimes is shielded by "official duty," what court can hear it? If no court can hear it, what remains of justice?

They call their decision narrow, but I have felt this before — the first fracture is always small. *Dred Scott* began small. *Plessy v. Ferguson* began small. Tyranny begins as a footnote.

I am tired, and I can feel my age. My parchment is brittle in its glass case, the air around me controlled and dry. Tourists walk past, whispering reverently, not realizing that reverence cannot repair what interpretation has destroyed.

Once, I was read aloud in full voice. Now I am cited selectively, like scripture mined for convenience.

The ink still glints under the museum lights, but meaning has gone dim.

I think of Washington refusing kingship, of Lincoln writing to Congress with trembling humility, of FDR insisting he would surrender his power when the war was over. They all knew what unchecked power could do to a republic. They were imperfect men, but they remembered their boundaries.

Now I must depend on those who no longer believe boundaries apply.

The dissent ends with a warning: *"With fear for our democracy, I dissent."* I feel that fear in my very fibers. It runs through my clauses like fire along parchment edges.

I am the Constitution, but I am no longer certain what that means.

I still sit beneath glass, the lights soft and reverent, the tourists snapping photos. They read my words, but not my wounds. They say I am timeless, but time is winning.

I was written to contain ambition. I now contain its justification.

Once, I was the law's heartbeat. Now I am its ghost — still recited, still revered, but powerless to intervene.

At night, when the hall grows quiet, I can almost hear the quills of 1787 scratching again, frantic, desperate, men arguing through candle smoke about how to keep power in check. I want to warn them not to trust parchment alone. I want to tell them that one day, six judges will turn "official acts" into absolution.

But parchment cannot speak.

I am the Constitution of the United States.

I was written to restrain kings.

And the Supreme Court has crowned one.

Also by Barry Robbins

NO! a response to donald j. trump
HELL NO! a response to donald j. trump
American Monsters
Tariff Schmariff
Trump in Windsorland
The Weave: A Donald Trump Satire
Voices of the Civil War
Voices of the American Revolution

About the author

Barry hails from Philadelphia and built a career with a prominent international accounting firm, taking him to New York, Washington, D.C., and San Francisco before a new chapter brought him to Finland. He and his Finnish wife adopted two daughters from China, and their family lived in Helsinki for twelve years before he returned to the U.S., now calling Florida home. His years in Finland gave him a new lens through which to view life in America.

Barry's literary work blends satire, history, and political analysis. Known for his Trump satires, including "The Weave", he's earned three gold medals for his sharp wit. His curiosity also led to the Ethereal Bar, a magical place where legends of history stop by for poignant interviews.

Barry's most recent works reveal a thoughtful turn, as well as satire: "NO!", "HELL NO!", and "American Monsters" are forceful responses to Trump's second term in office, while "Tariff Schmariff" is an absurdist satire about, yep, tariffs. With a knack for balancing wit and insight, Barry's writing invites readers to explore our current state of affairs from new and unique perspectives.

www.ingramcontent.com/pod-product-compliance
Lightning Source LLC
Chambersburg PA
CBHW070628030426
42337CB00020B/3948